CAGE AND
GARDEN BIRDS

CAGE
and
GARDEN
BIRDS

Georg Steinbacher

LONDON
B. T. BATSFORD LTD

636.686
STE

English Language edition
First published in 1959

Translated
by Peter Gorge

MADE AND PRINTED IN GREAT BRITAIN BY
WILLIAM CLOWES AND SONS LTD., LONDON AND BECCLES
FOR THE PUBLISHERS
B. T. BATSFORD LTD
4 FITZHARDINGE STREET, PORTMAN SQUARE, LONDON, W.1

CONTENTS

LIST OF ILLUSTRATIONS

8

9

A BIRD-TABLE ON THE WINDOW-SILL

We can obtain great pleasure from birds, even in winter, if we know how to attract them. A bird-table can be quickly made from simple materials: a few boards, nailed together and varnished, with a roof covered in roofing felt. It is most important to protect the food from wind, snow and rain; the birds must have easy access and enough room, and we should also be able to have a good view of them. The bird-table should therefore be placed directly against the window—without a rear wall—and the front left open to give the birds easy access. The roof must project on all sides to protect the food. The bird-table should be at least 20 in. deep and 12 in. wide, so that the less aggressive species can also reach the food. Then a seed ring should be hung up on a piece of string, some grain placed on the ground, and the bird-table will be ready. It should be cleaned out every day and the soiled

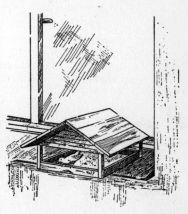

Bird-table for the window-sill, with roof and open sides

food replaced. It is most important that food should be supplied during hard frosts. During long cold spells the birds suffer heavy losses, and some species are apt to become nearly extinct over large areas.

Most of the commercial bird foods can be improved with sunflower, hemp or maw seed, since they are mostly made up from the cheaper and less nourishing seeds, which are quite adequate for sparrows or greenfinches, but not for other birds.

Be careful about giving potatoes, bread or other left-overs. Most of it is bad for the birds, particularly in a frozen state. Feeding rings are easily made at home. Simply render down some beef suet, add bird-seed and pour the liquid mass into a round cardboard box. When its contents have hardened, the box—without, of course, its lid—is hung up for the tits. To make a suet ring, arrange two boxes concentrically and pour the suet into the gap.

Seed ring

What birds can be expected to appear on the bird-table? This depends on the district. In the city, with hardly any gardens, little more than sparrows, some coal-tits and marsh-tits and perhaps a few greenfinches will come. Blue-tits, nuthatches, bramblings and chaffinches need parks and large gardens. Blackbirds and robins can be tempted with the dried berries of the mountain ash, crumbs and insects.

The prospects are somewhat better near open country, where the tree-sparrow, a smaller version of the house-sparrow, perhaps the great spotted woodpecker or the lesser spotted woodpecker, and the bullfinch might appear.

If the bird-table is placed in the garden, on top of a pole—always within sight of the window—jays might come to it. Great care must be taken to protect the birds from cats. There must be no cover for them to creep through and they must not be able to climb up to or jump at the birds.

Your labours will be well rewarded from the first frost to the beginning of spring. But do not

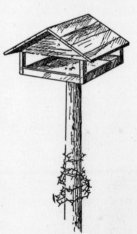

Bird-table on a post for the garden

expect the garden to be freed from insect pests, merely because the birds have been helped through the winter. Certainly, birds will keep pests down to some extent. Undoubtedly, bird-tables and other feeding places will save many a species from local extinction during hard winters. After all, the birds have not been kept alive merely for the sake of a few extra cabbages or apples. Even sparrows should not be resented. What little damage they do in fields or gardens, annoying at the time, is really negligible. And remember that they feed their young entirely with insects during the summer. Therefore do not disturb them at the bird-table and, instead, enjoy watching them settle comfortably next to the fast-moving tits.

Colour plate 1 on p. 21 shows the most important winter visitors. The description—as for all other plates—is on the opposite page. It includes the country of origin of each species and the colour of the female (♀), where different from the male (♂). The dimensions always refer to full length, from the tip of the beak to the tip of the tail, with fully outstretched neck.

With the approach of spring, the garden should be made ready for the birds. What can be done to encourage them? For birds breeding in hollows, put up nesting-boxes. It is advisable to put up two for each expected pair, so that the birds can choose. Such boxes are supplied by many firms and can also be made at home without any great knowledge of carpentry. They must be easy to put up, easy to remove and easy to open while on the tree, so that they can be checked to see that all is well inside.

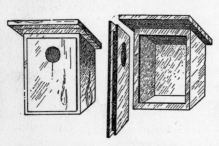

Wooden nest-box. Right: the front has been removed for checking

This, of course, should only be done if there is any reason for anxiety, since the birds must not be disturbed unnecessarily. Nesting-boxes must be large enough, and the round hole must allow the parent birds to get in and out comfortably. In the case of blue-tits and willow tits, the diameter should be at least $1\frac{1}{8}$ in.; for coal-tits, nuthatches, flycatchers and redstarts $1\frac{3}{8}$ in.; for starlings and wrynecks at least 2 in. The inner measurements of the nesting-boxes should be $4\frac{3}{4} \times 4\frac{3}{4}$ in., with a height of $9\frac{3}{4}$ in., and 6×6 in. and 10 in. respectively. To attract even larger birds, such as tawny owls, make the nesting-boxes correspondingly larger. Nesting-boxes for wagtails must have a slit *c.* $1\frac{5}{8}$ in. wide immediately below the roof in place of the round opening. The wood for home-made boxes must be strong and well seasoned and should be nailed together very carefully. The roof should project about an inch above the opening, should slant towards the back and must be covered with roofing felt. The nesting-boxes should hang as straight as possible, must be at least 8 ft. above the ground and should face east or north-east, so as not to be exposed to the prevailing winds which, in England, mostly come from the south-west. The outside will have to be creosoted against the weather, and the front must be easy to detach. Since all bought nesting-boxes are constructed in this manner, simply copy their design. The boxes are removed in autumn, repainted, the roofing felt is replaced, and all the remains of the nest are cleared out, since these provide a breeding ground for lice and other vermin, which would attack any bird that ventured near the box in the spring. The nesting-box might, in any case, have become too full for any more nests during the breeding season.

Nest-box with square opening for wagtails

For birds breeding in hedges, other nesting facilities must be provided. The hedge round the garden must be pruned hard to grow as thick as possible. It will then provide shelter and support for many nests. Unfortunately, most hedges are given a square trim and thus grow thin at the base, where the branches cannot get enough light. To prevent this, it is necessary to prune to the shape of a pyramid. The lower branches will then remain alive and thick with foliage. Free-standing shrubs should be trimmed frequently for the same reason. The resulting forks in the branches will provide good support for the nests. If as many birds as possible are desired in the garden, plant conifers, especially the species with many closely set branches, such as the Serbian spruce and the tiger-tail spruce. Being evergreens, they will give the birds protection when other trees are still bare.

Square-trimmed hedge

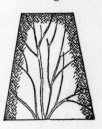

Correct pyramid trim

When hedges and shrubs are planted, be patient until the

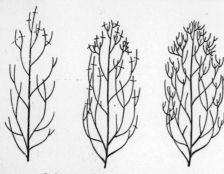

A frequently trimmed shrub grows very thick and gives excellent protection

foliage is thick enough to hide the birds completely, for they will only then feel really safe. Certain shrubs, such as dogwood, are disliked by birds. They prefer Philadelphus (Mock Orange), snowberry, forsythia, snowball, spiraea, viburnum, cotoneaster or deutzia. Favourite hedges are barberries (the Berberis species), whitethorn, hawthorn, quickthorn, beech, ilex, tree of life and spruce. Juniper hedges have an almost magnetic attraction for certain birds. Although the choice of shrubs will to some extent depend on the soil, there still remains a vast selection for almost any climate.

Overgrown walls also form good nesting grounds. Ivy, as an evergreen, gives good protection throughout the year, but is apt to damage the walls with its tentacles. Vines and climbing cotoneasters are also suitable but unfortunately remain bare in winter; they have no harmful effect on walls.

Fallen leaves under bushes should not be removed, for they provide an important source of food for thrushes, nightingales and robins. Many a gardener may see in such leaves an offence to tidiness, but he will have to put up with it if he is keen on birds.

Birds must have somewhere to drink and will fly to places where they can find water several times a day, especially in summer. Such journeys often take them far away, and we must therefore give them somewhere to drink in the garden. An old motor tyre, split in two and filled with water, is suitable but hardly beautiful. A sunken concrete or stone trough looks better. Running water, in a shallow stone or concrete bed, is better still; but any bird-bath must be well exposed, so that cats cannot approach it under cover.

A tyre, split open lengthways, makes a cheap trough

Assuming that the garden is ready, the hedges and shrubs are in leaf, the climbers trailing along the walls and the nesting-boxes in position, what birds can be expected during the nesting season? Sparrows will build their nests in recesses and crevices in the walls. Amongst them will be an occasional redstart, whose song can be heard in the early morning, before that of any other bird, until well into October. The redstart also settles in the eaves, projecting beams or in thick ivy. Both redstarts and sparrows will nest on the house rather than in the garden.

A concrete drinking trough with a stone in the centre

Chaffinches will come to the smallest garden and will be content with only a few small trees. They build their nests in the forks of branches and look for food on fairly exposed ground. Greenfinches are more particular. They need bigger trees and larger gardens. The blackbird, undoubtedly the finest of our native songsters, will thrive in the heart of the city, where there are few trees and scarcely more than a few square yards of grass. The song-thrush needs more space for its first brood of the season. The warblers like thick hedges. One of the smallest, the lesser whitethroat, needs comparatively little space, its larger relatives, such as the garden warbler and the blackcap, far more. The blackcap likes shrubs in the shadow of tall trees, the garden warbler also nests in more exposed bushes. Robins and nightingales, two of our best songsters, prefer well-shaded shrubs, particularly if last year's fallen leaves have not been cleared away. The former occurs throughout the British Isles, the latter likes warmth and is rarely found further north than the south of Yorkshire. Yellow buntings, linnets, hedge-sparrows and the red-backed shrike, or butcher bird, all like thick hedges, if these are on the edge of open country or near woods. The wren thrives in copses, gardens and thickets and builds its spherical nest in grass banks, the forks of branches, and the hollows and eaves of buildings. Its clear and penetrating song can also be heard in winter. If a garden is overshadowed by tall trees, it might also have goldfinches and an occasional siskin. Near extensive parks or woods a cuckoo might even be seen. The hen comes quite close to buildings when she is looking for somewhere to lay her egg. The only bird of passage amongst the doves, the turtle-dove, frequently visits gardens, as does the wood pigeon. Both must be considered pests rather than welcome visitors.

Bullfinches and hawfinches also make their homes in gardens. The bullfinch prefers low thickets of conifers, the hawfinch taller, deciduous trees.

Who are the likely inmates of the nesting-boxes? House-sparrows, unfortunately, are amongst the first to settle, especially in towns. It will hardly be possible to avoid ejecting them, together with their large nests. Boxes with openings up to

1⅛ in. diameter are suitable for the two smallest tits, blue-tit and marsh-tit. The larger coal-tit and the nuthatch need openings at least 1⅜ in. wide. Each pair of tits has two broods per season; the nests are easily recognisable from the white eggs, speckled reddish-brown. Spring without the song of the tits, the whistle of the nuthatch, can hardly be imagined. The pied flycatcher is a rare visitor to our gardens, although it is quite common in some parts. The male, in contrast to the obscure greyish-brown female, looks very striking in his black-and-white plumage. Starlings need even larger nesting-boxes. Although useful destroyers of insects, they are not well liked near orchards where they can do much damage in summer and early autumn. They usually have two nests.

The tree-sparrow, a smaller and prettier relative of the house-sparrow, is found in the country and the more sylvan suburbs. It also builds a spherical nest. The tree creeper, who dwells in woods and parks, will use the nesting-box if a small slit is made in the rear wall in place of the hole in front. If the garden is large and fairly quiet, it might attract some wood-peckers. The lesser spotted woodpecker likes fruit trees and conifers, where it hollows its nest out of the decaying wood. The green woodpecker is a larger kind and therefore needs somewhat harder wood to support its nest. The wryneck is a close relative of the woodpecker, but does not climb trees in the same manner. It lives on insects, especially ants, and usually nests in the holes of rotting trees. But it also uses holes made by woodpeckers and nesting-boxes of the type suitable for star-lings. The wryneck, once a fairly common garden bird, is now very rare.

Pied wagtails, black redstarts and spotted flycatchers like to nest in holes and prefer nesting-boxes with a wide slit under the roof in place of the small orifice. But they will occasionally use ordinary nesting-boxes and may also build their nests under the eaves, on projecting beams, amidst the ivy or in an old hole in a brick wall.

Do not be surprised if many birds use the most unlikely places for their nests, however lavishly they may be provided with nesting-boxes. Tits and redstarts are fond of letter boxes

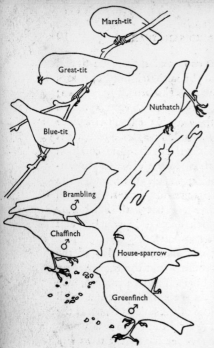

Marsh-tit, *Parus palustris.* 4½ in. British Isles, Europe and Asia, from the Altai region to Japan. Many varieties. **Great-tit,** *Parus major.* 5¾ in. British Isles, Asia, north-west Africa. Many varieties. **Blue-tit,** *Parus caeruleus.* 4¼ in. British Isles, Europe to Syria and Persia, north-west Africa. Many varieties. **Nuthatch,** *Sitta europoea.* 5½ in. British Isles, Europe to China, north-west Africa. Many varieties. **Brambling,** *Fringilla montifringilla.* 5¾ in. The bird in the illustration is in his winter plumage; the feathers on head and back turn black in spring. They are greyish-brown in the female, whose throat and chest are somewhat duller; her colouring is altogether less bright. Northern Europe, northern Asia, from Norway to eastern Siberia; in England only a winter visitor. **Chaffinch,** *Fringilla coelebs,* 6½ in. Tail and wings are alike in male and female, the back is dark olive-brown, the breast a brownish-pink. British Isles, Europe and western Asia. **House-sparrow,** *Passer domesticus,* 6¼ in. The female without a black throat; the nape and the edges of the wing feathers are light brown, rump and breast a brownish-grey. British Isles, Europe, northern and central Asia and India, North Africa. Introduced to America and Australia. **Greenfinch,** *Chloris chloris.* 6¼ in. The female less conspicuously green and yellow, rump and breast more grey, the back more brown. British Isles, Europe, western Asia, north-west Africa.

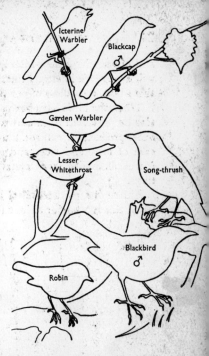

Icterine Warbler, *Hippolais icterina.* 5½ in. Central Europe to western Siberia, northern Caucasus. **Blackcap,** *Sylvia atricapilla.* 5¾ in. In the female, the crown is rufous-brown. British Isles (summer visitor), Europe to western Siberia, Asia Minor, north-west Africa. Several varieties. **Garden Warbler,** *Sylvia borin.* 6 in. British Isles (summer visitor), Europe, western Siberia. **Lesser Whitethroat,** *Sylvia curruca.* 5¼ in. British Isles (summer visitor), western Europe to eastern Asia and Pakistan. Several varieties. **Song-thrush,** *Turdus ericetorum.* 8½ in. British Isles, Europe to western Siberia, Asia Minor. Several varieties. **Blackbird,** *Turdus merula.* 10 in. In the female, the back is a dark greyish-brown, throat and breast are light brown or greyish-brown with darker patches, the rump is greyish-brown, the bill mostly dark brown. British Isles, Europe to central Asia and China; north-west Africa. Several varieties. **Robin,** *Erithacus rubecula.* 5¾ in. British Isles, Europe to western Siberia; Asia Minor, north-west Africa. Several varieties.

and of watering cans which have been left hanging about, and will even settle in empty tins. The birds will choose what suits them best, regardless of our plans for them.

When the birds have been attracted to the garden, they must also be protected from crows, magpies, jays, cats, weasels and other predatory creatures. Shooting is out of the question in the case of cats, and trees and nesting-boxes must therefore be surrounded with sharp metal spikes, as shown in the illustrations.

Although a garden full of birds means a certain amount of work, this is a labour of love that will be amply rewarded.

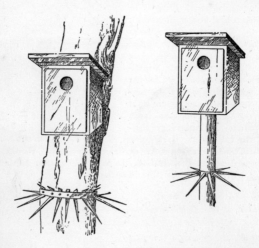

Nest-boxes. Left: on a tree; right: at the top of a post. Both have been protected with iron spikes against cats.

CAGES AND AVIARIES

Often, a young bird may be found which has left its nest too soon and is now at the mercy of all kinds of enemies. But we cannot help unless we know how to rear it and what to do when it has grown up. Suitable accommodation comes first. A small cage is best for a single bird, and larger numbers will go into a box-type cage or an aviary. Very few people can afford to put entire rooms at the disposal of their birds.

There are many types of cages on the market, but most of them are of rather unsuitable design. Manufacturers are often obviously badly advised and their products are often made on purely 'decorative' principles, without any regard for the needs of their inmates. Very few firms make really adequate cages. Since most cages are also very expensive, many bird-lovers will try to make their own. Instructions are given below.

One of the most common types is the open wire cage. Its sides and roof are made of wire bars, its base of sheet metal. The bars are galvanised, or painted with a durable metal varnish against corrosion and to prevent the accumulation of dirt and vermin. The gaps between the bars must be sufficiently narrow to prevent the birds from pushing their heads through and hurting themselves. The base should be fairly high, at least 2 in., otherwise sand, remains of food, etc., will spill into the room. The base will also contain a metal drawer, covering the bottom of the cage; this drawer is filled with a thick layer of sand. It should be as high as possible and should slide in at the front of the cage; otherwise, it might easily buckle. A flap in front of the opening will stop the birds escaping when the drawer is pulled out. The front of the cage should also contain a sliding wire door, with further openings—also to be closed with sliding wire panels—for feeding and drinking troughs. These can also be fitted at the sides. Often, cages are made of a hardwood frame, with only the bars made of metal. Such cages are not very satisfactory. The wood, in any case, must be

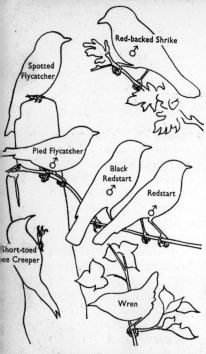

Red-backed Shrike, *Lanius collurio*. 7 in. The back of the female is reddish-brown, underparts a light fawn, with grey markings. British Isles (summer visitor), Europe to western Siberia and Pakistan. Several varieties. **Spotted Flycatcher,** *Muscicapa striata*. 5¾ in. British Isles (summer visitor), Europe to central Siberia and Pakistan. Several varieties. **Pied Flycatcher,** *Muscicapa hypoleuca*. 4¼ in. The back of the female is dark brown, without the white patch above the beak, underparts light grey. Both sexes look alike in winter plumage. British Isles (summer visitor), Europe, western Siberia. Several varieties. The male of the closely related Collared Flycatcher (*Muscicapa albicollis*) has a white collar. (Breeding range: Asia Minor, to eastern France and Poland.) **Black Redstart,** *Phoenicurus ochruros*. 5¾ in. Wings and back of the female dark grey, the underparts somewhat lighter. British Isles, Europe to Siberia and North West Frontier Province, north-west Africa. Several varieties. **Redstart,** *Phoenicurus phoenicurus*. 5½ in. British Isles (summer visitor), Europe to central Siberia and Persia, north-west Africa. Many varieties. **Short-toed Tree Creeper,** *Certhia brachydactyla*. 5¼ in. Western Europe to Asia Minor, north-west Africa. Many varieties. The very similar Tree Creeper, *Certhia familiaris*, has a somewhat shorter beak and also occurs in the British Isles, northern Europe, North America, China and Japan. **Wren,** *Troglodytes troglodytes*. 3¾ in. British Isles, Europe, Asia, North America. Many varieties.

---

well varnished, or it will warp and tear and become a breeding ground for parasites.

Many birds—especially soft-bills—will be happier in box-cages, which consist entirely of wood, except for the front and the base. Such cages will give better protection against cold and draughts and will also give a feeling of security to birds who normally nest in hedges. They need the dark and love to

Greater Spotted Woodpecker, *Dryobates major*, 9½ in. The female without the red nape patch. The crown is black in the adult and red in the young bird. British Isles, Europe to northern Asia and China. Many varieties. **Lesser Spotted Woodpecker,** *Dryobates minor*. 5½ in. In the female, the crown is a dull white. British Isles, Europe to northern Asia and Korea, Asia Minor to Persia, north-west Africa. Many varieties. **Cuckoo,** *Cuculus canorus*. 13 in. Some females are reddish-brown instead of grey. British Isles (summer visitor), Europe, Asia, Africa. Several varieties. **Wryneck,** *Jynx torquilla*. 6¾ in. British Isles (summer visitor), Europe, northern Asia, north-west Africa. Several varieties. **Turtle-dove,** *Streptopelia turtur*. 11¼ in. British Isles (summer visitor), Europe to Turkestan and Pakistan, North Africa. Several varieties. **Collared Turtle-dove,** *Streptopelia decaocto*. 11½ in. South-eastern Europe to Korea and China. Several varieties. It has moved further north in recent years and has occurred in Austria since 1943, and in Germany since 1946.

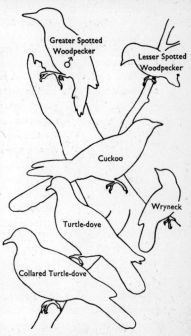

Greater Spotted Woodpecker ♂

Lesser Spotted Woodpecker

Cuckoo

Wryneck

Turtle-dove

Collared Turtle-dove

feel that they can withdraw there from real or imaginary enemies.

Box-cages, too, must have a door and openings for feeding and water troughs in the wire panel. It is best to make this

panel completely detachable, so that the cage can be thoroughly cleaned. The wood on the inside must be given several coats of a good light-coloured paint to show up the birds. The outside is also painted. Under no circumstances must any paint be used which contains lead, since birds always nibble at the bars and would thus poison themselves.

Such cages are quite unsuitable

Paint and varnish close the pores of the wood and prevent splitting and warping. This will keep out parasites, such as red-mite. The box-cage, too, will need a sand-filled metal drawer. It is best to fix slightly raised hardwood battens to the bottom of the cage, otherwise it might jam against grains of sand, etc.

Every cage also needs a bath, which is best fixed in front of the opening for the door.

Perches can be bought in any pet shop, or can be made at home. The spacing is most important. They must be sufficiently

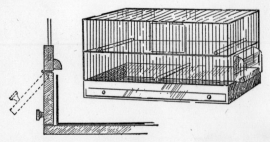

Wire cage. Left: cross-section through the base, showing tray and trapdoor

apart to force the bird to jump as far as possible with the help of its wings. Water and food must never be kept under a perch, where they might get fouled. They must also be far enough from the ends to allow clearance for the bird's tail. One perch should be placed fairly high near each end of the cage, a third is put further down in the middle. The two upper perches should be as wide apart as possible, since caged

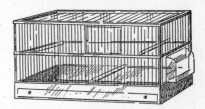

Wire cage with hardwood frame

birds like to be high up and will jump across from one perch to the other. They will go to the lower perch when they want to eat or drink. For a wire cage, a groove is cut into each end of the perch, which is then simply held by two opposite bars. Fitting perches to a box-cage is slightly more difficult. A groove has to be cut into one end—for the wire in front—and the other end has to be fitted with a dowel or a spike to go into a hole in the wall at the back. But it is better to make perches that can be easily removed. Two metal discs, with two rubber discs between them—as shown in the illustration—will hold the perch in position, if they can be screwed into the wood. The lower perch may be left out in smaller cages; in larger cages two extra perches can be fitted near the feeding and drinking troughs. It would be unnecessary, in this case, to have openings for these

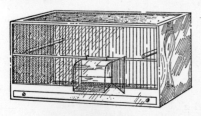

Cage for soft-bills. It has a wire front and wax-cloth sides and back

troughs in the wire panel. Simply put them on the floor of the cage, taking care that they are not immediately under a perch.

If the birds have very tender feet, the bottom of the cage should be covered with moss or peat, instead of sand. The peat must be kept slightly damp, since the birds will otherwise raise a lot of dust. Sponge rubber mats and sponge-like synthetic materials have also proved very useful; they can be washed in hot water.

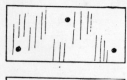

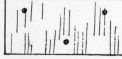

Rooms will stay very much cleaner if the lower part of the cage is surrounded by a strip of glass. This will prevent sand, food and water from being thrown about.

Cages should be as large as possible; the bigger they are, the more the birds can move about and the healthier they will be in consequence. Length matters more than anything else. The cage should be

Two arrangements for perches. The lower is more suitable

at least five times as long as its inhabitant, in any case not less than 20 in. wide, 12 in. deep and 14 in. high. Cages for slightly larger birds, such as starlings, must be at least 30 in. long and proportionately wider and higher. Ground birds need a long cage without a perch. This should be at least 28 in. long for birds no bigger than a lark, but need be no more than 12 in. high. All ground birds love to take wing in sudden spurts and their cages—of the box type—will therefore need a wax-cloth roof to prevent injury.

Cages intended for several birds must be correspond-

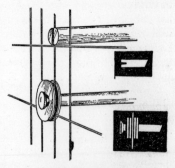

Perches. Top: fitted with a groove; bottom: fitted with a special device and held in position between the bars

ingly larger. Again, remember that most birds like to move upwards, thus mostly using the upper portion of the cage. It is therefore pointless to build tall cages over a narrow base, since the area used by the birds would still be very small. Length and width must be increased proportionately. Here, too, the upper perches have to be spaced as widely apart as possible to make the birds use their wings. The lower perches must be placed to prevent the birds above from fouling those below. In place of one large drawer, two smaller ones will be needed, since these can be handled more easily; the gap between them must be covered, so that nothing can fall into it. It is not advisable to replace perches with branches and twigs. They are very difficult to choose and to fit accurately, are hard to clean, and will cause fouled drinking and feeding troughs. Ground birds, such as quail, etc., should never be kept with birds who like to soar upwards, if they are not to get rather dirty. Finally, see that there are enough perches. Each bird must have its own sleeping place and should not have to fight for it.

Flight-cage for one breeding pair, several pairs, or a number of birds of the same species

Where should a bird-cage be placed? All birds need a lot of light. Their cages will therefore be put near the window, where they can enjoy the sun for some time during the day. But they must be protected from excessive heat, no less than from draughts. Sudden changes in temperature—as a result of opening the window, etc.—are also harmful. It is therefore best to put cages on shelves; in the case of wire cages, these can be protected with a piece of material. Most birds dislike cages on the floor intensely, because human beings appear disproportionately large and frightening from there. The best position is slightly below eye level.

If sufficient space is available, an indoor aviary can be made for groups of birds or for breeding pairs. It will be rather like a small-scale outdoor aviary. The most suitable materials are

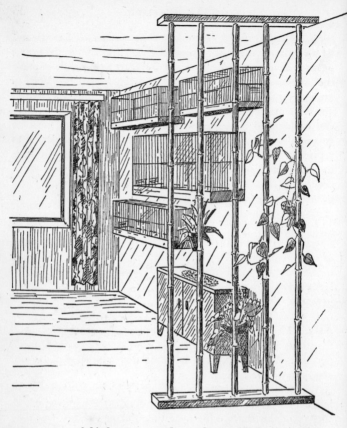

A bird-room must have plenty of light

angle iron or sheet metal, unless hardwood is preferred. The frame is covered with galvanised wire-netting, which must be close meshed in the case of smaller birds (not wider than $\frac{5}{8}$ in.). Here, too, a base of sheet metal or wood is needed, with two drawers. The feeding troughs are best put on the floor. Again and again it must be remembered that height matters less than width and length and that cleanliness is more important than anything else in the care of birds. In a large cage, too, every corner must be easily accessible for cleaning.

The perches must be smooth and easy to clean. A profusion of twigs only causes the plumage of the birds to suffer and is out of place in an indoor aviary. We must keep our love of greenery under control, lest we transform the aviary into a miniature jungle with potted plants, turves, branches and bark. It may all look very well for the first few hours, but the plants will soon wither, the leaves will get soiled and the sand will be impossible to clean. The birds will also get frightened, if we 'arrange' things in the cage too often. It cannot be over-stressed that the cage must be easy to clean and easy to survey, so that sick birds can be noticed immediately. There must be no shelter for vermin, and there must be no unbidden guests.

A well-equipped aviary near the window

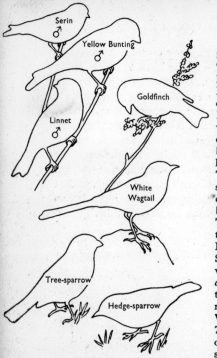

Serin, *Serinus canarius.* 4½ in. The female is a less brilliant yellow, and more streaked below. Mediterranean to the Baltic. It has occurred as a vagrant in the British Isles, Denmark and Finland. Two varieties, one of which is the ancestor of the Canary. **Yellow Bunting,** *Emberiza citrinella.* Also known as Yellow-hammer, 6½ in. The female less yellow and more streaked. British Isles, Europe to central Siberia. Several varieties. **Linnet,** *Carduelis cannabina.* 5¼ in. The female without red markings, the underside more streaked. British Isles, Europe to western Siberia and Pakistan. Several varieties. **Goldfinch,** *Carduelis carduelis.* 5 in. British Isles, Europe to central Siberia and Pakistan, north-west Africa. Many varieties. **White Wagtail,** *Motacilla alba.* 7½ in. In the female, the crown is often grey. British Isles (a rare summer visitor), Europe, northern Asia and southern China, north-west Africa. Many varieties. **Tree-sparrow,** *Passer montanus.* 5½ in. British Isles, throughout Europe and central Asia to Japan and south-east Asia. Many varieties. **Hedge-sparrow,** *Prunella modularis.* 5¾ in. British Isles, Europe, Asia Minor to Persia. Several varieties.

Starling, *Sturnus vulgaris.* 8½ in. British Isles, Europe to central Asia and North West Frontier Province. Many varieties. **Nightingale,** *Luscinia megarhynchos.* 6½ in. Southern England (summer visitor), western Europe and North Africa to Asia Minor and Turkestan. Several varieties. The very similar Thrush Nightingale is darker in appearance and has a brownish-mottled breast. It occurs throughout eastern Europe to western Siberia. **Whitethroat,** *Sylvia communis.* 5½ in. British Isles (summer visitor), Europe to central Siberia, Asia Minor and north-west Africa. Several varieties. **Marsh Warbler,** *Acrocephalus palustris.* 5¼ in. British Isles (summer visitor), Europe to western Siberia, Asia Minor. **Tree Pipit,** *Anthus trivialis.* 6 in. British Isles (summer visitor), Europe to central Asia, northern Caucasus and Himalayas. Several varieties. **Woodlark,** *Lullula arborea.* 6 in. British Isles, Europe to southern Russia, north-west Africa. Several varieties. **Skylark,** *Alauda arvensis.* 7¾ in. British Isles, Europe and Asia, America to Japan and Ceylon. Many varieties.

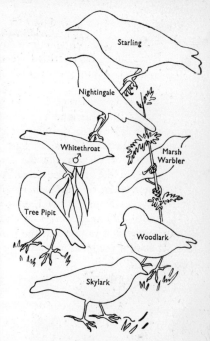

Even mice have settled in comfort in indoor aviaries. A 'natural' setting gives the birds no pleasure and means a lot of work.

This applies especially to glass cages. These are a fairly recent introduction. The front simply consists of a pane of glass. The birds quickly get used to it and can be observed much better. The sides must be made of wire to allow for proper ventilation, but the advantages of the three-sided box-cage are lost in consequence. A glass-fronted cage must also be much wider than any other type, since the pane has to be some distance from the perches. It would otherwise get very dirty and would need almost constant cleaning. It must in any case be possible to pull out the pane and to replace it with a wire panel, if the birds are not to be thoroughly frightened by one's

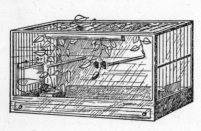

Glass-fronted cage

arm during cleaning. Such a cage is often lit from below, equipped with plants and put away from the window into the middle of the room. What should be a comfortable home for the birds is thus turned into an expensive and laborious 'decorative' feature, which can only be justified if the owner can spare a lot of time and cash or if he keeps sugarbirds and humming-birds, who feed on nectar and would therefore appreciate flowering plants in their cages.

A room where the birds can fly about in freedom is every bird-lover's dream, a dream that will only very rarely materialise to-day. But many older houses have light basements and these can easily be transformed into bird-rooms; many attics are also suitable. First of all it is necessary to put a frame of close-meshed wire-netting in front of the window, so that the room can be aired without the birds escaping. If the bird-room faces east, west or south it will be all the better. The entrance must also be protected to prevent the birds getting out when a person enters with full hands and is unable to close the door fast enough. A wire porch with a separate door which is closed before the door of the room proper is opened, will be the best solution.

If there is no central heating, any stoves, pipes, fire-places, electric fires, etc., must be guarded with wire-netting or the birds might get very badly hurt.

The floor should be given several coats of liquid lino and

A bird-room. The corner at the back, on the right, has been equipped as a nesting-place for foreign finches

should also be sized. All gaps between the boards must be closed carefully. In a basement room, with a concrete or stone floor, this will present no problem. When the floor is absolutely dry, it is covered with a thick layer of sand. The door must be absolutely draught-proof and must not let in any air when it is closed. It has to be protected against rats and mice with a 20 in. wide strip of sheet metal at the base. Both are greatly attracted by the smell of bird-seed and will try to get

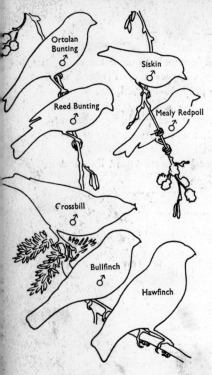

Ortolan Bunting, *Emberiza hortulana.* 6½ in. The crown of the female more brown, with darker stripes, otherwise paler, with mottled throat and breast. Europe to Pakistan and western Mongolia, north-west Africa. **Siskin,** *Carduelis spinus.* 4½ in. The female without black chin and crown, underparts a dirty white with darker streaks, the wings the same as in the male. British Isles, Europe, western Siberia, China, Japan. **Reed Bunting,** *Emberiza schoeniclus.* 6 in. The head of the female is brown, with darker patches, no white collar. The underparts duller, with darker streaks. British Isles, Europe to China and Japan, Asia Minor. Many varieties. **Mealy Redpoll,** *Carduelis flammea.* 5 in. Only the male has a pink breast; m. and f. otherwise alike. The red gradually fades to yellow in captivity. The British variety, the Lesser Redpoll *Carduelis flammea cabaret,* is smaller and browner. British Isles, northern Europe, Asia, North America, Alps. **Crossbill,** *Loxia curvirostra.* 6½ in. The female without any red, with yellowish rump and underparts, otherwise a dark-greyish mottled-brown. British Isles, Europe, northern Asia, North America, north-west Africa. The young males are yellow instead of red. **Bullfinch,** *Pyrrhula pyrrhula.* 6½ in. The northern variety is distinctly larger. The female grey instead of red, with greyish-brown back. British Isles, Europe to China and Japan and northern Persia. Many varieties. **Hawfinch,** *Coccothraustes coccothraustes.* 7 in. British Isles, Europe, northern Asia to North West Frontier Province. Several varieties.

---

in with great perseverance. Rats are a terrible menace to birds and can wreak havoc in a single night. Even mice will attack some smaller species. Nestlings are completely at their mercy. Wooden floors should be protected against damp with

Hartort's Scimitar Babbler, *Pomatorhinus schisticeps.* 10 in. The female somewhat duller. Himalayas to Thailand and Annam. Several varieties. **Black-headed Sibia,** *Leioptila capistrata.* 10 in. North-western Himalayas. **Plumbeous Thrush,** *Turdus plumbeus.* 10 in. Cuba, Bahamas, Antilles. Several varieties. **Grey-and-orange Ground Thrush,** *Turdus citrinus,* or *Geokichla c. citrina.* 8½ in. The female somewhat duller. South-east Asia, from India to Indo-China and the Malay Peninsula. Many varieties. **Common Shama,** *Copsychus malabaricus.* 10 in. The female a dark greyish-brown instead of black, breast light brown. Southern Asia, from Pakistan and Ceylon to Java and Borneo. Several varieties. **Magpie (or Straits) Robin,** *Copsychus saularis.* 7½ in. The female dark grey or brownish-grey instead of black. Pakistan to China, Ceylon to Malaya and Philippines. Several varieties. The two last-named birds in the illustration come from India.

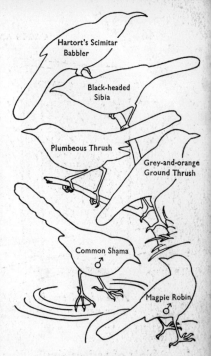

Hartort's Scimitar Babbler

Black-headed Sibia

Plumbeous Thrush

Grey-and-orange Ground Thrush

Common Shama ♂

Magpie Robin ♂

---

roofing felt, on which sand can be put directly. It is also possible to use hardboard or plasterboard and cover this with an inch-thick layer of concrete, first making sure that this will not prove too heavy in an attic room. The walls are painted in a light washable distemper or simply whitewashed several times a year. This is the easiest and cheapest solution. Ground birds, and birds that love digging, should be given flat white metal dishes, filled with pieces of turved lawn. These can be kept damp in their containers and will therefore last much longer. Moss, too, is very popular.

Perches might be replaced by branches in such a room; but exchangeable perches, which can be cleaned easily, are preferable. Here we must repeat once more that all perches or

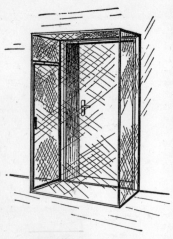

An enclosed porch of wire-netting for the bird-room door

branches must be kept where the birds cannot soil the walls. Branches can also dangle from ropes on the ceiling. Large, flat metal dishes, filled to a maximum depth of $\frac{3}{4}$ in. to prevent the birds from drowning, will serve as baths and drinking troughs. Place boards in these dishes, so that the birds can reach the water comfortably and without having to perch high up on the edge. Food should be provided in as many small bowls as possible—the more the better—so that each bird has somewhere to eat, even when it is chased away by a bully. It is important to separate birds of various sizes during feeding, since larger birds will often leave nothing for others. This can be prevented by placing small wire guards—whose bars are too closely spaced for the larger, but not for the smaller birds—over some of the bowls.

Nesting- and sleeping-boxes should be fitted to stands and not to the wall. They can be bought in pet shops or made at home. A round hole or a slit immediately under the lid will serve as the entry. Many birds like small roller travelling-cages for nesting. Surrounded with evergreen twigs, they will be less conspicuous and will give the birds a

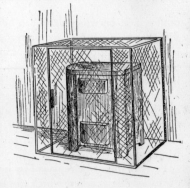

Stove with wire guard

greater feeling of security. Birds normally nesting in hedgerows should have a corner of the room cut off with a wide-meshed wire frame and filled with privet or gorse. The birds can easily enter through the wire and will then build their nests in the branches. The twigs should be changed when they get too dirty. Birds nesting in trees will need tree branches, hung close to the ceiling. Two-tiered wire frames filled with sturdy, dry rushes are ideal for birds nesting on the ground.

Roller travelling-cage

The electric light for the aviary— if the owner has to go there after dark—must be guarded with wire-netting. It is, of course, better to have the light in the wire porch. Great care must be taken when the light is switched off, since the birds— who will have left their perches —may flutter around excitedly, thus creating havoc. It is best to fit a delaying device, which causes the light to go out gradually, thus giving the birds enough time to find sleeping places. Birds which normally travel at night should have a low-voltage lamp, giving a weak light, near their aviary so that they can find their way about when they feel restless.

Frame for rushes

The number of birds has to be kept rather low if the aim is to combine aviary and conservatory, or the plants will suffer. It must be possible to spray or wash the leaves fouled by the birds. This excludes a wooden or paved floor. Many bird-lovers have therefore planned their conservatory as an annexe,

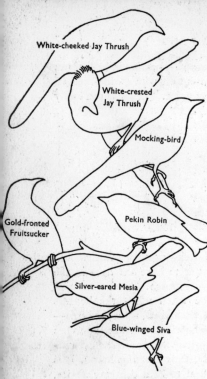

White-cheeked Jay Thrush

White-crested Jay Thrush

Mocking-bird

Gold-fronted Fruitsucker

Pekin Robin

Silver-eared Mesia

Blue-winged Siva

White-cheeked Jay Thrush, *Garrulax chinensis.* 10½ in. Southern China, Burma. Several varieties. **White-crested Jay Thrush,** *Garrulax leucolophus.* 11½ in. Himalayas to Sumatra, China and Formosa. **Mocking-bird,** *Mimus polyglottus.* 9½ in. U.S.A. to Mexico and the Antilles. Several varieties. **Pekin Robin,** also called **Red-billed Leiothrix,** *Leiothrix lutea.* 6 in. The female somewhat duller. Northern India, northern Burma, southern China, northern Indo-China. **Silver-eared Mesia,** *Mesia argentauris.* 6¾ in. The female duller. Northern India, northern Burma and Indo-China to Sumatra. Several varieties. **Blue-winged Siva,** *Siva cyanouroptera.* 5½ in. Himalayas to southern China, southern India. Several varieties. **Gold-fronted Fruitsucker,** *Chloropsis aurifrons.* 8 in. The female somewhat paler. From Pakistan throughout India to Indo-China to Sumatra. The bird in the illustration comes from southern India, and other varieties are imported less frequently.

overlooked by one or two of the living-room windows. The floor, in this case, is simply the earth. Any surplus water sinks in and provides nourishment for the plants. Nectar feeders and sugarbirds, who are attracted to blossoms, can do very well under these conditions. But such aviaries are expensive to install and to maintain, since they require constant heating.

Living plants are altogether not suitable for aviaries if they cannot be looked after properly. They soon die and become unsightly when the birds pick off the leaves, bark and shoots for their nest.

Having provided a suitable home for the birds, whether aviary or cage, then decide on the choice. The beginner should

Scarlet-chested Sunbird, *Nectarinia senegalensis,* also called *Chalcomitra senegalensis.* 5½ in. The female quite inconspicuous, with black throat, underparts yellowish-white, mottled with black. African grasslands and steppes, from Senegal to the White Nile and South Africa. Many varieties. **Yellow-winged Sugarbird,** *Cyanerpes cyaneus.* 4¾ in. The female dark green above, olive-green below. Male in non-breeding dress resembles female. Tropical America from Mexico to southern Brazil and Bolivia. **Pitpit,** *Dacnis cayana.* 5¾ in. Back and wings of the female greenish-yellow, underparts somewhat lighter, with bluish-green head and grey throat. Northern South America to Nicaragua. Several varieties. **White-eye,** *Zosterops palpebrosa.* 4 in. From India and Ceylon to the Philippines, southern China to Indonesia. Several varieties.

Scarlet-chested Sunbird ♂

Yellow-winged Sugarbird ♂

Pitpit ♂

White-eye

White-cheeked Bulbul

Golden-vented Bulbul

Red-whiskered Bulbul

White-cheeked Bulbul, *Pycnonotus leucotis,* also called *Molpastes l.* 7¼ in. Persia to western Pakistan. **Golden-vented Bulbul,** *Pycnonotus cafer,* also called *Molpastes haemorrhous.* 8 in. From India to Indo-China and Java. Many varieties. **Red-whiskered Bulbul,** *Pycnonotus jocosus,* also called *Otocompsa emeria.* 8 in. India to Indo-China, southern China to Malacca. Several varieties.

---

stick to varieties that present no great difficulties and require only the most elementary knowledge. Such birds exist amongst most groups. They can be found amongst seed-eaters and soft-bills, which include song-birds, parrots, quails or members of the pigeon family. The prospective bird-keeper must also make up his mind whether he wants his birds for their song, as pets or for breeding. It must be remembered that only the male of the species sings, and mainly when he is kept on his own, because his song serves to attract the female. If a person wants a bird to be particularly friendly, it is also advisable to keep it without company, since birds in pairs or groups will find their social life amongst each other. Many bird-lovers will prefer to keep to birds of one group only. Everybody will have to form his own judgment, preferably before any expensive mistakes have been made.

In England, as in most civilised countries, birds are protected by law. No British bird can be kept in captivity unless it is cage or aviary bred, nor can it be sold unless it is closed ringed. We must therefore buy most of our birds. Cage-bird societies and the fanciers' journals will gladly help in the choice of a supplier.

Birds can, of course, be bought by post. The right choice will matter even more than normally in this case. If the bird should arrive dead, the dealer and carrier must be told about it immediately.

There are several points to remember. Birds that are very calm in the shop, birds that distend themselves when they feel unobserved, thus giving their feathers a ruffled look, birds sleeping in daylight and, especially, birds that can easily be caught, are highly suspect. All of them are probably very ill. Less reputable dealers like to protect themselves against losses by getting rid of these 'tame' birds first. All birds must therefore be examined very carefully before purchase. Pick up the bird carefully, as shown in the illustration, blow against the breast feathers to make sure that the breast is firm and fleshy and examine the legs, which might be deformed, broken or excessively horny, thus indicating old age. If there is obviously nothing wrong, pack the bird and take it home as quickly as possible. Transporting birds needs some skill. For short journeys, a cardboard box with air-holes is extremely suitable, because the bird cannot damage its feathers on hard walls or bars. Parrots will need a more solid container, since they bite their way out of cardboard; a small hardwood box is best for them. For longer journeys, birds need travelling-cages, i.e. wooden boxes with doors of wire-mesh or metal bars, a perch and containers for food and water. There should be a sponge in the water-bowl to soak up the water and to prevent spilling. The travelling-cage is then wrapped in brown paper, which is pierced in several places to let in air. If the cage were not wrapped, the birds would get too excited. Then mark the parcel clearly 'LIVE-STOCK WITH CARE' and despatch

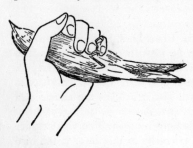

The proper way to hold a bird for examination

it as quickly as possible. In England, live animals are usually sent by rail. There must not be too many birds in the cage, nor must breeds that do not get on together be mixed. They should not differ too much in size, or the smaller birds might get squashed against the walls. In winter, only send birds used to low temperatures, and even these will be in danger if they have previously been kept in a warm, heated room. Larger birds must have a good meal on the day before the journey and should then be sent off in the evening, to arrive at their destination in the morning; they can manage a few hours without food, even in daylight. Smaller birds must never be without food, since they eat very often, though only small quantities. They could easily suffer serious damage to their health if they had nothing to eat for any length of time.

A conscientious dealer will only sell birds that have been fully acclimatised. Nevertheless it is essential to take great care. The new arrival is placed into a cage of its own, before it is

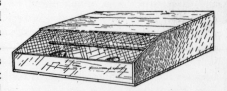

Travelling-cage for smaller birds

allowed to join the other birds in the flight-cage, bird-room or aviary. If the bird is very frightened, cover its cage at first with a piece of slightly transparent cloth—loosely woven linen, a thin tea-towel, etc.—and try to move about very gently. The bird will be greatly comforted if it is spoken to often, because the human voice has a soothing effect on all creatures.

The morning is the best time for collecting the bird from the shop. It can then get used to its cage in daylight and will settle somewhere to sleep when the evening comes. It is most important to choose the right moment for introducing new-comers to cages or aviaries. Old residents will sometimes not accept a new bird and will chase it all round the cage. Therefore take time and watch the situation, so that you can intervene if necessary. If peace does not return, take the established birds out of the cage and put them somewhere else for a few days. The new bird can then settle down, and will defend itself when the earlier inmates return. It is most important to make sure that the newcomer will eat and drink. Birds used to small cages often find it very difficult to settle in large aviaries and may starve to death amidst well-filled bowls of food and water, because they cannot recognise them for what they are. If it looks as though this is going to happen, move the bird to a cage which, though bigger than its previous home, is much smaller than the aviary. It will thus get used to its new sur-roundings more gradually.

All British song-birds will have been bred in captivity, since the catching of wild birds has been illegal since 1934. There may be some difficulty in getting indigenous birds from breeders, but it is well worth the trouble. Siskin, goldfinch and lesser redpoll are all easy to keep and can be highly recommended to any bird-lover. Indeed, this applies to most finches. Most seedsmen stock a special finch mixture, which can be improved by adding one part maw seed to five parts of the bought mixture. It is important that these smaller birds with their delicate beaks should have small-grained foods. Birds with tougher beaks, such as greenfinches and bramblings, have sunflower seeds instead. A very good mixture can also be made from four parts of teazle seed, three parts canary seed, two parts hemp and one part linseed. This mixture can be varied for different species by adding chopped walnuts, rape and niger seeds. Smaller birds would be given more maw seeds, and larger birds more sunflower seeds. A regular supply of green stuff, such as chickweed, dandelion, shepherd's purse, etc., and an occasional piece of fruit will be of the greatest help in keeping the birds well and happy. Bought hemp seed can be crushed for the smaller birds, who are often unable to crack the husks themselves. But no more than twenty-four hours' supply must be crushed, because the crushed seed becomes rancid very quickly, and rancid or—even worse—mildewed food is bad for any bird.

If several birds of the finch family are kept in one cage, see that they are all cock birds, otherwise some birds will pair up and fight the rest.

The cage for a single bird of the size of a siskin must be at least 16 in. long, 8 in. wide and 10 in. high. Cages for chaffinches should be no less than 20 in. long and those for hawfinches 30 in. long, with corresponding increases in height and width.

Siskins are amongst our most popular native cage-birds, for

their song and cheerful disposition, rather than for their plumage, which is not particularly bright. A siskin will also quickly take to its master, especially if it is kept on its own. Left to fly around the room occasionally, it will find its way back to its cage if it can expect fresh food on its return. Its relative, the lesser redpoll, is rather brightly coloured in freedom, but not in captivity. Like the redpoll and siskin, the goldfinch is a good climber, although it may not manage to dangle from the roof of its cage quite as skilfully as they do. Its plumage does not suffer in captivity. Since male and female are rather alike, it is necessary to get the dealer to guarantee that the bird being purchased is a male. Some hens may sing occasionally, but the majority will not. Both siskin and goldfinch need a lot of maw in their food.

The linnet is less keen on climbing about its cage. It is chiefly loved for its beautiful song. Like the redpoll, it will lose its red marking in captivity. Very few breeders have managed to produce the attractive red tinge. In parts of Germany, singing competitions are held for linnets and people will travel long distances to enter their birds. Food must not include too much oily seed, especially hemp, or the birds will become fat and lazy.

The crossbill, too, is a keen climber. His song is not outstanding, although rather pleasant. He also loses his red plumage and turns yellow in captivity. Next to hemp-seed, crushed oats and sunflower seed, he appreciates fir cones more than anything else. He will bite whole fir cones to pieces and may even keep his red colour on such a diet, especially if he is also given fir buds.

The serin, a small, agile bird, is the closest wild relative of the canary, with which it will readily cross. It has settled over large parts of Germany, where it had been unknown during the last fifty years, but has not been observed in freedom in the British Isles. It has an attractive song.

The bullfinch, one of our most handsome birds, will keep most of his colour if he is well fed. Like crossbills, bullfinches love the buds of trees and shrubs, which they should be given as special treats. The song of the cock is not very conspicuous.

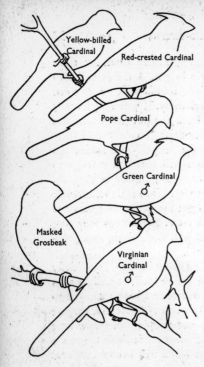

Yellow-billed Cardinal, *Paroaria capitata.* 6½ in. South-western Brazil to northern Argentine. **Red-crested Cardinal** (also sometimes called **Grey Cardinal**), *Paroaria coronata,* or *cocullata.* 7½ in. Southern Brazil to Argentine and Bolivia. **Pope Cardinal),** *Paroaria larvata,* also called **Dominican Cardinal,** *Paroaria dominicana.* 7 in. North-eastern Brazil. **Green Cardinal,** *Gubernatrix cristata.* 7½ in. The female much duller, with some greyish-white. Southern Brazil to Argentine. **Masked Grosbeak,** *Eophona personata.* 8 in. China and Japan. **Virginian Cardinal,** *Pyrrhuloxia cardinalis,* also called **Virginian Nightingale,** *Cardinalis cardinalis.* 8½ in. The female duller, with dark red tail and grey face. The male loses his bright red colour in captivity. U.S.A. to Mexico. Several varieties. In the past, Virginian Cardinals were mostly imported from the U.S.A., where they are now protected. They now usually come from Mexico.

In some parts of Germany, breeders rear the young bullfinches by hand to teach them to sing certain tunes, which are whistled to the birds before they have even left their nests. As soon as they can be separated from their parents, the cocks are put into separate cages—if possible even in separate rooms—where nothing can divert their attention. They must not hear any other bird or music of any kind. The same tune is then whistled to a bird many times per day—preferably all day—until he has eventually learned all, or most, of it. This happy stage should be reached by the beginning of February. Some German bird fanciers will pay high prices for such creatures.

The bullfinch, though almost lethargic in his cage, is remarkably lively when allowed to fly around the room. The

American Goldfinch, *Carduelis tristis.* 4½ in. In the female, the crown is dark olive brown, back brownish-yellow. North America. Several varieties. Yarrell's Siskin, *Carduelis yarelli,* from eastern Brazil has an olive-green back and yellow wing patches; the Arkansas Goldfinch, *Carduelis psaltria,* 4½ in., is completely black above. **Red Hooded Siskin,** *Carduelis cucullata.* 4¼ in. The female dark grey above, with grey cheeks and throat, red breast and rump. Northern Venezuela. **Pileated Finch,** *Coryphospingus pileatus.* 5½ in. The crown of the female is brown, without the crest. Eastern Brazil to Columbia. **Cuban Finch,** *Tiaris canora.* 3¾ in. The female duller, with brownish and pale yellow head. Cuba. **Olive Finch,** *Tiaris olivacea.* 4¼ in. The female duller. West Indies, Central America, northern parts of South America. **Guttural Finch,** *Sporophila nigricollis,* also called *S. gutturalis.* 4¼ in. The female much duller, with white cheeks, dark brown tail. Wings edged with olive, underparts dirty white. Northern parts of South America, Leeward Islands. **White-throated Finch,** *Sporophila albogularis.* 4¼ in. The female grey-black, except for the tail. North-eastern Brazil, Guiana.

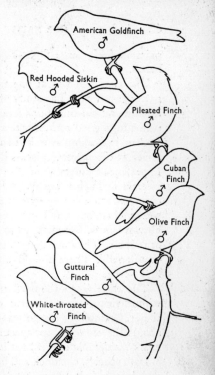

hawfinch, as the biggest member of his group, needs a comparatively large cage. Apart from seeds and buds, he loves the contents of cherry-stones, which he cracks without difficulty with his strong beak. He can peck very hard and must therefore be handled with great care. His song is insignificant, his plumage extremely attractive.

Few birds are easier to keep than greenfinches. Like hawfinches, they are rather pretty, but are poor singers. Being somewhat querulous, they should be kept to themselves in pairs in fairly large flight-cages, where they will frequently breed.

The chaffinch was at one time amongst the most popular native cage-birds. The study of finches was almost a science of its own and old-time finch fanciers, especially, would pay high prices for a good cock. There are still singing competitions for finches, in London as well as some German towns. Enthusiasts arrive at the meeting places, their charges in darkened cages. Experienced judges then give their opinions. Elsewhere, the interest in finches has flagged. Few people are interested in cage-birds that can be seen in every park or garden. Yet many young chaffinches fall out of their nests and thus get into human hands. But chaffinches are never as friendly as siskins or redpolls. They will do well in captivity and may even breed occasionally. There should not be more than one pair per flight-cage.

The brambling—the northern cousin of the chaffinch and a winter visitor—has a pretty colour, but is no outstanding singer. Bramblings like to make use of their strong beaks and should therefore be kept apart from other birds. They will live to a considerable age, if kept in flight-cages or aviaries.

Both species, chaffinch and brambling, must be given berries and insects in addition to seed and green stuff during the summer (q.v. Insect-eaters, p. 71). This is essential for their health, since they eat a lot of insects under normal conditions.

All finches—except for the hawfinch—use insects to raise their young, and they must therefore have suitable food in their aviaries for rearing. Fresh and dried ants' eggs, soaked soft foods, chicken meal, etc., are all readily accepted. When the fledglings are a little older, add dry, crumbly cream cheese—this must be absolutely fresh—which is also an excellent food for soft-bills. Later, gradually get the young birds accustomed to seeds. The older birds should have the half-ripened seeds of grasses, weeds, etc., and the berries of shrubs and trees added to their food as often as possible. Bullfinches and greenfinches are very fond of the berries of the mountain ash.

Now for the most popular of all caged finches, the canary! Our highly bred birds are very different from their insignificant looking wild ancestor. The Canary Islands, in the Atlantic, were captured by the Spanish navy in 1478. Spanish sailors brought the little bird to Europe. It was well established in Germany one hundred and fifty years later. Canaries were at

first bred chiefly in the Tyrol, later in the region of the Harz mountains. Many interesting varieties were produced, especially during the Rococo period of the eighteenth century. Some of these breeds were distinguished by peculiar shapes and colours, ruffs, crests, etc. In Britain to-day about ten varieties of canaries are kept, the most popular being the 'type' birds. In Germany the most popular canary is the roller, whose song is priced above everything else. The budgerigar has frequently replaced the

Wire baskets for nests

canary, but thousands of young birds are still raised every year and exported all over the world. In the Harz region, the work of centuries has produced the 'Harz Roller', whose song bears little resemblance to that of his earliest ancestor.

Breeding canaries is not very difficult. In winter, the hens are kept together in a spacious flight-cage or bird-room; they need light and sun and protection from frost. Their principal foods are sweet rape seed and a seed mixture, consisting of two

parts canary-seed and one part made up of niger seed, linseed, and a little hemp. They also need some green stuff. At the beginning of April, place each hen

Testing eggs

in a separate breeding cage, which should be 16 in. long, with a height and width of 12 in. In addition to ordinary food, it must now be given special egg food. This is made by mixing a finely chopped hard-boiled egg with a small teacupful of biscuit or bread crumbs. Each hen gets half a teaspoon per day. For nesting, hang a small box-cage on the outside of the

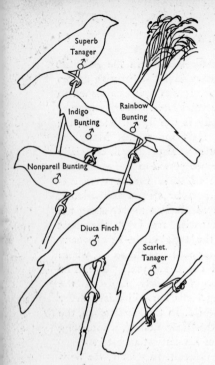

Superb Tanager, *Tangara fastuosa*, also called *Calliste fastuosa*. 5½ in. The female duller, with more blue on the head. Eastern Brazil. **Indigo Bunting,** *Passerina cyanea*. 5 in. The female is brown above, with banded light reddish-brown breast, and buff underparts. North and Central America. The Lazuli Bunting, *Passerina cyanea amoena*, a species of Indigo Bunting from the North American West, has a reddish-brown breast and white underparts. **Rainbow Bunting,** *Passerina leclancherii*. 5¼ in. The female a dull olive above, with yellowish-olive head and yellowish underparts. Southwestern Mexico. **Nonpareil Bunting,** *Passerina ciris*. 5½ in. The female green above, with darker crown, and yellowish-green, with reddish reflections, below. U.S.A. to Panama and Cuba. **Diuca Finch,** *Diuca diuca*. 7 in. The female duller, with more brown. Chile. **Scarlet Tanager,** *Rhamphocoelus brasilius*. 7¼ in. The female dark brown above, with some red on the crown, reddish breast, and somewhat lighter below. Brazil.

---

larger breeding cage or put one of the wire baskets, obtainable for this purpose, into the cage itself. Cow-hair, thread picked from cotton rags, etc., must also be placed in the cage, so that the hen can make her own lining for the nest.

In Germany, one cock is used for several hens. This involves getting the birds accustomed to each other—by no means always easy, since they can be quite quarrelsome—and separating them immediately after mating. This process has to be repeated daily until an egg is produced. English breeders prefer breeding cages divided by wire panels. The birds will get used to each other gradually and can be placed safely into one cage as soon as they start feeding each other. This means

Black-headed Bunting, *Emberiza melanocephala.* 7½ in. The female dark-streaked olive-brown above, with yellowish rump and dirty white underparts. South-eastern Europe to Persia. **Red-headed Bunting,** *Emberiza bruniceps.* 7½ in. The female greyish-brown with darker streaks above, underparts yellowish-white, rump yellowish. Persia, western Turkestan. **Saffron Finch,** *Sycalis flaveola,* also called *Sicalis f.* 5¼ in. The female less yellow and more brownish-grey above, with grey throat. South America, as far as northern Argentine. **Golden Sparrow,** *Passer euchlorus,* also called *Auripasser e.* 5 in. The female yellowish-grey above, with pale yellow breast and white belly. Aden Protectorate, Red Sea coast. **Sudan Golden Sparrow,** *Passer luteus,* also called *Auripasser l.* 5 in. The female a dirty cream above, cheeks and underparts yellowish-white. Sudan, East Africa.

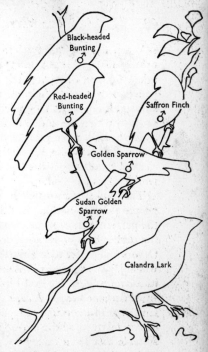

Black-headed Bunting ♂

Red-headed Bunting ♂

Saffron Finch ♂

Golden Sparrow ♂

Sudan Golden Sparrow ♂

Calandra Lark

Calandra Lark, *Melanocorypha calandra.* 7¾ in. Mediterranean to Turkestan.

---

that each cock will only have one hen, but it saves a lot of trouble and is far kinder to the birds.

The first two eggs—each hen lays between three and five, usually one per day—are carefully removed and stored, until the third appears. They are then put back into the nest. As soon as the hen starts incubating, omit egg food and feed her exclusively on seed, especially rape. After a week, examine the eggs by holding them against the light: fertile eggs will appear opaque, others should be discarded. The young will hatch after a fortnight. Again, place egg food in the cage after they have hatched, so that the hen can feed them. They will be ready to leave the nest after three weeks, and should then be able to feed themselves.

When the young have left, the old nest is removed, more nesting material is put into the cage, and the cock is allowed to rejoin the hen as soon as she starts building a new nest. The young are put into a flight-cage, where the cocks will soon start singing. They must be gradually accustomed to crushed rape seed, to which are added at first some soaked teazle and later ordinary seed. Also, gradually introduce some green food. The hen will meanwhile have started laying again. Many experienced breeders suggest that hens should not have more than two clutches per year.

The English, fortunately, are a nation of animal-lovers. Some people think of nothing but the pleasure to be obtained from the performance of some creature, whether it is a seal balancing rubber balls on its nose, or a bird singing with all its might. Others will prefer their animals to be happy and contented and will enjoy the song of a bird only if they know it to be happy in its surroundings. No real bird-lover will place his charges in small darkened cages. A cage for a singing canary should be no smaller than an ordinary breeding cage. Clean, sweet rape seed, canary mixture, a little cut-up fruit and green food are the most suitable diet for a canary cock. To get enough calcium, both cock and hen should always have a cuttle fish shell in their cages.

Many breeders keep birds for their colour rather than their song. There has been considerable progress in producing birds of a reddish hue since it has been possible to cross the red hooded siskin with canaries. These hybrids have, in turn, bred quite freely. To-day, colour counts as much as song amongst competitors at exhibitions where experts will distinguish without any difficulty between shades of white, green, yellow and red, however much they may seem alike to the uninitiated. In England the song has no value with new coloured canaries at a show. The crossing of canaries with other finches is very popular. Crosses of canaries and siskins were already reported from Frankfurt in 1699: the tradition of cross-breeding is thus very old. In general, wild cocks are used with canary hens. Greenfinches, goldfinches and siskins have proved particularly successful for this purpose. The greater the difference between the parent birds, the more difficult it will be to produce hybrids, most of which prove sterile.

Other finches do not breed quite as easily as canaries, although the greenfinch—and, to a lesser degree, the bullfinch and the goldfinch—will breed quite successfully in captivity, if each pair is put into a pheasant enclosure, i.e. a very large aviary. They will not do so well in a bird-room, where the other inmates will probably disturb them. The chances would be better in a large cage—which should measure at least 40 in. × 16 in. × 24 in. Here, too, put a travelling-cage or a wire nesting-basket in a corner and mask it with evergreen twigs, unless the birds are exceptionally tame. The young are raised on chopped, hard-boiled egg, ants' eggs, mealworms, bread soaked in milk and a mixture of hard-boiled egg and crushed biscuits. Bullfinches will also need green twigs, whose buds they love. Greenfinches often raise their young on ordinary seed mixture and soaked hemp or sunflower seed; also add bread soaked in milk and ants' eggs. These foods must also be given when it is intended to rear the young birds by hand. Here, too, the young must not be removed from their parents until they can feed themselves, although they may have left their nest somewhat earlier.

The eggs of most finches can be entrusted to canary hens, who will raise the young as their own.

The buntings, too, belong to the finch family. All of them, yellow bunting—also called yellow hammer—reed bunting and cirl bunting, are very pretty, but make poor singers. In addition to seeds, they need more soft food during the summer than other finches.

House-sparrows and tree-sparrows make delightful indoor pets, if they are hand reared. They will need the same food as young siskins or goldfinches. Their diet must also include soft food, in addition to seed; sparrows need comparatively large cages to feel secure and happy. The tree-sparrow is attractively coloured, as is the male house-sparrow. The keeping of tits in captivity has been illegal all over Europe since 1910, with the exception of Britain. The authorities even have to be notified if we wish to put an injured tit into an aviary. The coal-tit is a very hardy bird with an attractive song. It is apt to be rather aggressive and should therefore be kept on its own. The more delicate blue-tit is generally—but not always—peaceful; the marsh-tit is even less eager for quarrels. All these tits must have insects and soft food during the summer, although they will survive on seed in winter. Two relatives of the *paridae*—as the tit family is called—are the tree-creeper and the nut-hatch. Both love running along tree trunks. The nuthatch will thrive on the same food as tits, the tree-creeper is purely an insect-eater. Both species need individual cages, which should measure at least 24 in. × 24 in. × 24 in. Back and sides of the cage should be lined with split, untreated branches, so that the birds can climb about.

Two European species of seed-eating pigeons are too large for cages, but not for the bird-room. These are the turtle-dove and the collared turtle-dove. These pigeons need the same food as finches, except that sunflower seed should be replaced by hemp. Collared turtle-doves lay up to five clutches of eggs per year, turtle-doves never more than two.

The quail, rather like a miniature partridge in appearance, is suitable for bird-room or cage. In the latter case, the cock will need a cage to himself; the roof must consist of a soft cloth, or the bird might hurt itself when it tries to fly. The cage itself must be at least 40 in. × 12 in × 16 in. There is no need for perches, but the tray must be much deeper than usual and must be filled with sand to the rim. The bird will also need its daily square of freshly turved lawn to nibble at. The bowls for food and water are placed on the ground. Quails need a very fine seed mixture: hemp, millet, maw, huskless oats, etc., and a soft mixture of ants' eggs, semolina and grated carrot. They will occasionally breed in the bird-room if the hen has several hiding-places to choose from for nesting. A pair of quails or, at the most, one cock and two hens are installed, and are not separated unless the cock starts attacking, as he sometimes does after the eggs are laid.

The young are reared on the same food as pheasants (p.166).

To keep British birds is not always easy, if they are to stay well and happy. It is now forbidden to offer any wild bird for sale, unless it has been bred in a cage or aviary, in which case it must be ringed as soon as possible. This will generally be when the bird is between six and nine days old.

Robin and warbler, nightingale, blackbird and shrike are soft-bills or insectivorous birds, needing soft food, and many of them, such as the reed warbler, will only thrive on individual attention. A diet, adapted to the need of each bird, is the beginning and end of keeping soft-bills. Each expert, here as in most other fields, has his own methods, by which he swears.

The beginner should gain some experience with seed-eaters, before trying his hand at soft-bills. The real bird-lover does not consider his pets merely a source of entertainment and he would not keep them unless he felt that he could look after them properly. It is his great pride to cater for all their needs, and to keep them alive and well for as long as possible.

In freedom, soft-bills feed mainly on insects, adding other food according to season; thrushes and warblers will eat berries, wrens fine seed. Some birds, like flycatchers, will touch nothing but insects. Their digestive system is chiefly adapted to animal protein foods, which they must be given in captivity.

Ants' cocoons (they are wrongly but usually called ants' eggs) are the most natural food for soft-bills, because they contain everything needed by the birds. Newly collected, fresh ants' eggs are best. In Germany, these are not easily obtainable, since the red ant is protected. Its cocoons (eggs) can only be collected with special permission from the authorities. In England, there is no such law, but the red ant is not very common and the 'eggs' of other ants will therefore have to be used. The chapter on pheasants contains particulars about obtaining 'ants' eggs' (p. 167). Often, we shall have to rely on bought dried eggs. The fresh eggs are thinly spread out—or they will spoil—on a piece of newspaper and are stored in a cool place. They can also be kept in a deep freeze, but must be thoroughly thawed and warmed in this case before they are fed to the birds. Dried larvae can be damped with cold or hot water to make them more attractive.

Soft-bills also love mealworms. These are bred commercially and are easily obtained. We can also breed our own as follows: a one-gallon tin is filled with bran up to a height of roughly 6 in.; we then place a very flat bowl on the bran and fill this bowl every other day with grated raw carrot for the worms. Great care must be taken not to let any moisture get at the bran. Mealworms—about a jam-jarful—are put in and the tins are covered with lids of close-meshed wire and placed in a fairly warm room. Generation after generation of mealworms will be produced in steady succession, if there is enough warmth. To start with, we should reckon with a 'stud' of about a thousand mealworms in an 8 in. square tin. The bran has to be re-plenished all the time. If we have several boxes, worms can be taken from each, so as not to deplete the breeding stock. This will allow some of the mealworms to grow into beetles, which will lay eggs and thus supply us with more worms. The beetles can also be fed on potatoes, but here, too, we must be careful not to moisten the bran. The worms are given slices of bread to supplement their normal diet. Warmth and dry bran, plus freshly grated carrot, are the foundations of mealworm culture. The mealworms are killed and cut up; strong and healthy birds will also eat them alive. In all cases, they must be given as a tit-bit, in small quantities, because their hard skins are rather indigestible.

There are various other insect pests—such as the clothes-moth, the corn-weevil, etc.—whose larvae the birds will eagerly devour. Bird-lovers 'fortunate' enough to have beetles and cockroaches already breeding in their own houses will no doubt feed their offspring to the birds. Others, perhaps, may not be too anxious to breed what their wives are eager to exterminate. In that case, stick to mealworms and cater for other insect requirements via the pet shop.

The larvae of the red water flea and daphniae will have to

be bought, except in summer, when daphniae—also known as water fleas—can be caught with nets in stagnant pools.

Various other insects and caterpillars can be collected in field, forest or garden. The large brown cockroaches are very popular with birds, although they dislike the small black variety. Cockroaches are caught by placing hollow bamboo canes—or old gas tubing, etc.—in the rooms where these insects live. In the morning, empty the tubes into a bucket of hot water by tapping them against the sides. This will cause the cockroaches to fall into the water, thus killing them immediately. They are then fed to the birds. Many birds are fond of wood-lice. These occur in large quantities in damp basements, outbuildings or coalsheds. Birds who are fond of greenfly can be given branches covered with this garden pest; grasshoppers can be caught with butterfly nets; wasps' grubs can be bought or taken from their dwelling-places. Each bird-lover will discover his own sources of supply of live insects.

In winter, feeding the birds is more difficult and various substitutes will have to be used. Dried ants' eggs have already been mentioned. English bird-keepers like to use crushed puppy biscuits, best quality chicken meals, dried flies, silkworm pupae, etc. Many birds like finely ground raw beef, ox heart and boiled minced horse liver. Fresh, dry cream cheese—which we can make ourselves from milk—is an excellent food for all soft-bills, as is the chopped yolk of hard-boiled egg, although this is not quite so digestible. There are several patent egg foods on the market; these are finely ground before feeding. An egg-loaf can also be made from wheat flour, yolk of egg and fat. Ground rusks, soaked in milk, are very suitable for the larger species; poppy flour, with its high fat content, will make a welcome addition. Dry food mixtures are moistened with grated carrot or grated apple, both of which are always good for birds.

Birds eating berries and other fruit in addition to insects can be given chopped apples and pears, chopped bananas, soaked raisins and sultanas, boiled and cut-up carrots, ripe blackberries, redcurrants, black elderberries, the berries of mountain ash, juniper and yew, etc. The two last named, and elderberries, can be dried for the winter and soaked when they are needed.

The bird-lover will be able to make up a suitable diet for his charges from this list. If he would rather not go to such trouble, he will find a number of commercial foods for soft-bills. Dry mixtures are moistened with grated apple or grated carrot, 'fat' foods are given plain. But however good these mixtures may be, they have to be supplemented for the more delicate species and, indeed, for each individual bird. Here are some recipes for those making their own mixtures: the first consists of equal parts of ants' eggs, dried flies, and half-cooked minced ox heart, all mixed up with cream cheese. To this add a little grated apple or carrot, ground egg-loaf or yolk of egg. Another mixture—also for delicate birds—consists of one part each of dried flies, ground mountain ash berries and ants' eggs, and two parts each of boiled minced horse liver and cream cheese. If it is desired to make a really varied mixture for large numbers, use ½ lb. of egg powder, 5 oz. of dried ants' eggs, 5 lb. of biscuit flour, 3 oz. of charcoal, 12 oz. of dried flies, 6 oz. of fish meal, 6 oz. of calcium food, 12 oz. of milk powder, ½ lb. of coarsely ground silkworm pupae and 6 oz. of sultanas.

For the tougher breeds, mix ants' eggs, ground rusks, grated carrot and apple, and cream cheese in equal quantities. Larger birds, like thrushes, will do well on a mixture of two parts boiled rice and one part each of ground rusks, coarsely ground mountain ash berries, ants' eggs, boiled minced liver and any patent food for soft-bills.

If ants' eggs are not available, substitutes have to be used. Here are several recipes: No. 1 consists of cream cheese, finely crumbled egg-loaf or egg mixture, ground carrot. No. 2 is made up of cream cheese, finely crumbled egg-loaf or egg mixture, ground hemp seed, dried flies, grated apples, the sieved yolk of hard-boiled egg and scraped meat or ox heart. No. 3 is a mixture of cream cheese, powdered rusks, silkworm pupae, ground hemp seed and grated carrot. In each case, add mealworms as tit-bits and always give live or newly killed insects. Berries and fresh fruit are also essential, both for their vitamin content and because they provide variety. All soft food mixtures are easily spoiled in the warmth and must therefore be prepared twice daily from fresh ingredients. Never make more than is needed for immediate consumption. Such mixtures must feel soft and crumbly, never wet and sticky. Cod-liver oil and vitamin preparations can be added, but it is important to remember that a surfeit of vitamins can be quite harmful.

It is absolutely essential to check the health of the birds and to see that they do not become too fat or too thin. Although it will excite them, they have to be picked up from time to time for examination. The drawing (p. 54) shows how this is done. Thumb and index finger enclose the neck gently, but firmly, while the back rests on the flat hand. Then we blow against the breast feathers, thus exposing the skin over the breast-bone. The breast must be firm, the breast-bone must not stick out, nor must it be covered by a layer of fat. If the bird is too thin, its diet does not suit it, and experiments must be made until it is known what agrees with it. If it is too fat, feed more grated apple and carrot and omit or reduce fatty foods.

The needs of each species—and even of individual birds—may differ considerably. One experienced bird-keeper reports that his grey wagtail will only thrive on the best soft mixtures, another claims that his bird has been living for years on nothing but dried ants' eggs and ground hazel-nuts. Therefore it is essential to study the tastes of each bird.

Most of our song-birds are very lively and will therefore need comparatively large cages. These must be at least 24 in. long for the smallest breeds, and not less than 32 in. for thrush-sized birds. Most song-birds are quarrelsome and must therefore be housed separately. Box-cages with solid wooden sides and back will be found best. Only larks and starlings can have ordinary wire cages with open sides. If the birds are required to breed—by no means always easy—put them into large outdoor aviaries during the summer. Such aviaries must be suitably planted. Warblers need thick undergrowth, fly-catchers must have room to fly around, redstarts like open ground. Some soft-bills can be kept in pheasant runs with the other inmates, provided they do not breed close to the ground

—like robins and warblers—where their nests would be
destroyed by the larger birds. Their young are raised on live
insects and fresh ants' eggs. Outside the breeding season, song-
birds are kept in cages, where they can be fed individually—
especially during the moulting and migrating seasons—and
where they cannot fight.

All song-birds who move in big jumps, whether amidst
shrubs on the ground—such as nightingales and robins—or
from branch to branch—like warblers—must have resilient
perches to protect their legs. To prevent damage to the head,
the roof of the cage itself should always be formed by a wooden
frame, stretched with plastic or butter-muslin.

In winter, keep the song-birds in heated rooms, where they
will sing all the better. Birds who normally spend the winter
in the Tropics must not be kept in the cold, and even those
wintering at home must always be protected against frost.

The first soft-bill should be a starling. He is easily obtained,
and is hardy, friendly and amusing. His cage should be about
28 in. long, 16 in. wide and 20 in. high. Two perches will be
sufficient. Starlings are great eaters and make a considerable
mess. Their cages therefore need trays generously filled with
sand. Some bird-lovers prefer peat, but this is apt to leave the
room covered in dust and is therefore not recommended. The
starlings should be fed on a mixture of cream cheese, stale
bread or ground rusks soaked in milk, and a little scraped raw
meat, in addition to soaked bran, and a number of extras—
such as grated carrot, grated apple, dried ants' eggs and ground
insects—which ought to be varied as much as possible. One
or two mealworms should also be given as daily tit-bits. These
extras can also be added to a home-made or bought soft-food
mixture. A young starling will make a most attractive pet if
reared by hand. The young bird is taken out of the nesting-box
while still gaping for food. This should, however, not be done
until the feathers have begun to develop. He is then placed into
a little box, filled with hay—from which the excreta is removed
all the time, since the fledgling excretes as soon as he eats—
and is given at first fresh ants' eggs, a few mealworms and other
live insects. Gradually, he is accustomed to scraped meat and

boiled egg, later rusks are added, soaked in milk, and the normal starling food. At first, feed him hourly, later two-hourly, until the starling can feed himself. The females also sing and chatter, although not quite as much as the males.

The lark, a ground bird, prefers an open, sunny setting. Each bird is given a low cage, at least 28 in. long, with a width and height of 12 in. The base has to be fairly high, with a deep sand-filled tray. There should be no perches. A soft wax-cloth roof is of great importance, because larks rise horizontally when they are frightened. The cage is placed in a bright, sunny position. Since larks bathe in the sand, there is no need for a bathing trough. Food and water containers should be fairly deep and are best fitted to the outside of the base, thus allowing the bird to eat and drink through the bars, while keeping the food clean. In summer, give the larks soft food, with chopped green stuff and half-ripened seed; in winter add

Cage for larks, pipits and wagtails

maw seed, carrot seed, grass seed, millet, peeled oats and a few mealworms. Also place fresh grass turves in the cages as often as possible, so that the larks can peck at them, as they would in their natural surroundings. The two most popular varieties are the woodlark and the skylark, both noted for their song. Shelley's poem makes the lark especially dear to us. To keep such a bird in captivity would rightly seem little short of sacrilege. It is only young, injured larks that should be put into a cage, and then only for as long as is absolutely essential. The best food, under such circumstances, would be fresh ants' eggs, live insects, and stale rusks soaked in milk.

Wagtails and pipits are fast runners and also like using their wings. Their cage must therefore be at least as long as a lark's cage, with a height of no less than 16 in. It will also need two perches as substitutes for the branches where these birds love to settle in freedom. Wagtails should have a fairly large, shallow basin full of water, which must be replaced at least once daily, since they bathe and paddle a great deal. Pipits will be content with an ordinary bird-bath. Both should be given a good soft-food mixture, a few mealworms, live insects whenever possible, and fresh ants' eggs. Single wagtails or pipits can be kept in the bird-room; pairs would soon start quarrelling. The tree-pipit has a beautiful varied song; some wagtails occasionally imitate the voices of other birds. The condition of the feet is most important in larks, wagtails and pipits and must be watched constantly; the sand must be frequently changed and kept very clean.

The hedge-sparrow is a pleasant and hardy pet, who loves singing, and is easily tamed. It should be given a soft-food mixture, maw seed, some crushed hemp and a few mealworms. Its drab plumage explains why it is ignored by so many bird-keepers.

Thrushes are fine singers and have therefore always enjoyed great popularity. As large and strong birds, thrushes need big cages, at least 32 in. long, 16 in. wide and 20 in. high. The tray must be filled with sand to the brim and must be cleaned frequently. Peat, or a mixture of peat and sand, can be used in place of sand only, but it must be remembered that peat is rather dusty if it is not kept sufficiently damp. Thrushes will eat any of the soft-food mixtures already mentioned. Of good digestion and great eaters, they can be given the following cheaper mixtures: two parts cream cheese, two parts ground rusks, soaked in milk, two parts grated carrot, one part dried or fresh ants' eggs; or white bread, soaked in milk, ants' eggs, chopped meat and coarsely ground mountain ash berries. In addition, give them mealworms, cut-up fruit, raisins and sultanas, all kinds of berries and cooked, chopped carrots.

Young thrushes need fresh ants' eggs and live insects, as well as the above mixture. They must also have a little earth added to their food, although this is not necessary if they have chopped earthworms. Thrushes raised in captivity often do not sing as well as they would normally.

Breeding is fairly easy in large outdoor aviaries. In bird-rooms, thrushes are often rather aggressive against the other inmates.

The blackbird has a melodious song; the song-thrush, at times, sounds more repetitive and less continuous. The red-wing, the smallest common thrush, resembles the song-thrush, but can be recognised by its creamy eye stripe and rich chestnut flank. Its size makes it a suitable cage-bird, as does its song, which is not as loud as that of the other thrushes. The missel-thrush and fieldfare are too large and noisy for cages, although they were kept in captivity in the past.

The robin, one of the most popular cage-birds in Germany, is very friendly, needs little attention and sings very well. Beginners should start with a thrush, or a starling, and should then add a robin to their collection. Male and female look alike; since the hen frequently also sings, the sexes are very hard to distinguish. Give them the usual soft-food mixtures, or a special mixture of two parts grated carrot, one part dried ants' eggs, cream cheese, finely crumbled egg-loaf, ground mountain ash berries and hemp flour. In addition, robins should have fresh, or soaked dried, elderberries and a few mealworms. Robins will breed in a spacious cage, as well as in an outdoor aviary or bird-room. The difficulty consists in matching a pair, since robins are very hostile towards each other outside the breeding season. It is best to put the prospective partners into a cage, divided by a wire panel, like canaries (p. 64). The birds will then get used to each other and the moment the cock begins to feed the hen, they can be safely placed together.

Like the robin, the nightingale breeds in thick undergrowth, close to the ground. Here, too, it is mainly the cock which sings. Nightingales were at one time very popular cage-birds and many bird-lovers specialised in them. Innumerable recipes have been compiled, in addition to those already mentioned. One of the best-tried mixtures consists of two parts grated apple or carrot, and one part each of ants' eggs, maggots, cream cheese, egg-loaf and ground hemp seed; in winter, add a few mealworms, in summer fresh ants' eggs and as many live insects as possible. The cage for a single nightingale should be at least 24 in. long; the perches must be resilient and made of a soft material. As nightingales have very tender feet, put a piece of rubber sponge or synthetic rubber sponge—this must be washed daily in hot water—at the bottom of the cage in place of sand. Nightingales are kept in single cages, since they are hard to feed in a bird-room or aviary, where their diet cannot be given the necessary attention. Breeding has occurred in semi-captivity in fairly large enclosures.

The redstart, an interesting and lively bird, takes well to captivity, and quite a number have been bred in England. If a sick redstart is found and has therefore to be kept in a cage for a while, give it the same food as that given to nightingales. It also needs a lot of live insects. Redstarts do not get on together and must therefore be kept in individual cages. The male redstart is attractively coloured and has a pleasant song; the plumage of the black redstart is duller, and its song, too, is little more than a few short whistles, interspersed by croaks.

Flycatchers need a lot of room, because they are used to setting forth from buildings or tall trees; their cages should be at least 32 in. long. They, too, are fed on the same mixture as nightingales are given. Cages must never hold more than one flycatcher; pairs can be let loose with other species in aviary or bird-room. The song and plumage of the spotted flycatcher are by no means spectacular. The pied flycatcher is more handsome and a better singer. The collared flycatcher, distinguished by the whitish markings round its neck, sings better still, but is a very rare visitor to Britain. The diet of warblers differs very little from that of nightingales, except that they need a lot of berries, some chopped bananas, live insects and mealworms. They sing very well in separate cages, if we really can bear to put them into solitary confinement. The song of the rather inconspicuous garden warbler is sustained and beautiful. The blackcap with its glossy black crown looks more striking. Its song begins rather softly and increases in volume towards the end. The lesser whitethroat is a most attractive bird, with a very pleasant voice. Many whitethroats have only a simple song, although there are occasionally excellent singers amongst them. some of which will even imitate the voices of other birds. The blackcap has frequently bred in cage or aviary; male and female are distinguished by their crowns—black in the male, rufous brown in the female. Other warblers are often rather alike and are therefore not easy to pair.

Icterine and marsh-warbler are both reed-warblers; they are excellent songsters and have many admirers. The icterine warbler is very delicate and is extremely difficult to get safely through the moulting season, which occurs twice a year. Some authorities suggest feeding it on a mixture of two parts grated carrot, and one part each of ants' eggs, cream cheese, and scraped raw meat, in addition to fresh ants' eggs in summer and mealworms in winter; others give nothing but fresh ants' eggs in summer, and dried ants' eggs, supplemented by mealworms and grated apple, in winter; after New Year, for the winter moult, scraped meat, maggots, the yolk of hard-boiled egg and a little cod-liver oil are added. But the icterine warbler is a very rare vagrant in the British Isles and ringed specimens—the only birds we are allowed to buy or offer for sale—are not likely to be found in pet shops. The marsh-warbler has a remarkable song and, like the icterine warbler, mimics the voices of other birds. Both must be kept in individual cages and need the same food, including as many live insects as possible.

The red-backed shrike is also rather delicate. If we find a young bird that has fallen out of its nest, we can try hand-rearing with live insects and fresh ants' eggs. The adult bird is fed on a good soft mixture, made up of, say, one part each of dried ants' eggs, maggots, cream cheese, ground hemp, finely minced meat, as many live insects as possible and a few mealworms. It must have a cage of its own, because it will attack weaker inmates of the bird-room.

No small soft-bill is really hardy; all of them, from nightingale to shrike, must be taken into well-heated rooms before the onset of frost. Only the wren can stand lower temperatures. Its cage should have many perches, arranged diagonally so that the lower ones cannot get fouled. Since the wren likes to sleep in a sheltered position, place the nesting-box in the cage, where the bird may even build a nest during the breeding season, if it has the necessary materials. Wrens are fed on a mixture of dried ants' eggs, maggots, cream cheese, egg-loaf and minced lean

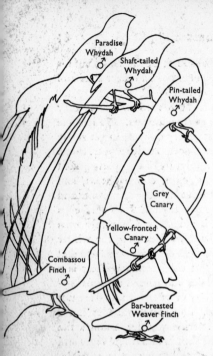

Paradise Whydah, *Vidua paradisaea*, also called *Steganura p.* The male in breeding dress, with tail, measures up to 14 in. The female light brown to light yellowish, with dark patches above, and two dark bands along the crown. Belly white, throat and chest reddish-brown, the flight and tail feathers edged yellowish-brown. In non-breeding dress, male and female are almost alike and only about 3 in. long. East, West and South Africa. Many varieties. **Shaft-tailed Whydah**, *Vidua regia*. Also called Green Whydah. The male in breeding dress is up to 12 in. long. The female has red feet, two dark streaks on the crown, otherwise light brown above, streaked with black. Throat yellowish-brown, underparts white. Flight and tail feathers edged yellowish-brown. Male in non-breeding dress like female. South Africa. **Pin-tailed Whydah**, *Vidua macroura*. The male in breeding dress with tail sometimes exceeds 12 in. Female resembles Shaft-tailed Whydah, but has reddish-brown feet. Male in non-breeding dress like female. Africa south of the Sahara. **Grey Canary**, *Serinus leucopygius*. 4¼ in. West Africa to Sudan. Several varieties. **Yellow-fronted Canary**, *Serinus mozambicus*. 4½ in. The female duller. African steppes and grasslands south of the Sahara. Many varieties. **Combassou**, or **Indigo Finch**, *Hypochera chalybeata*, also called *Vidua c.* 4½ in. The female brownish-grey above, with dark patches, two dark stripes along the crown, and wing coverts edged lighter. Belly and breast pale brown, shading gradually to white. Male and female alike in non-breeding dress. West Africa, from Senegal to East Africa and Lake Nyasa. **Bar-breasted Weaver Finch**, *Ortygospiza polyzona*. 3¾ in. The female a duller greyish-brown, with grey—instead of black—markings on head and neck. South and East Africa. The Quail Finch, *Ortygospiza atricollis*, a native of West Africa, lacks the white markings.

Cut-throat or **Ribbon Finch,**
Amadina fasciata. 5 in. The female
without the red band, the patch on
the belly not quite so marked.
South of the Sahara, from Senegal
to East Africa and the Transvaal.
Violet-eared Waxbill, *Granatina*
granatina. 5½ in. The female
greyish-brown above, with reddish-
brown head. Blue and purple
markings less distinct, underparts
yellowish-brown. South Africa.
The Purple Grenadier, *Granatina*
ianthinogaster, a close relative,
comes from East Africa and has
violet-blue underparts. **Red-**
cheeked Cordon Bleu, *Granatina*
bengala. 4¾ in. The female without
the red patch. Throughout Africa
south of the Sahara. The male of
the South African Cordon Bleu,
Granatina angolensis, lacks the red
patch. **Painted Finch,** *Cayleyana*
picta. 4¼ in. The female less red,
with more white markings below.
Central and north-western Australia. **Green-winged Pytilia,** *Pytilia*
melba. 5 in. The female without any red, head grey, throat light grey.
South, West and Central Africa. Many varieties. **Red-winged Pytilia,**
Pytilia phoenicoptera. 4¾ in. The female brown instead of grey. Africa,
from Senegal to Nile. **Peter's Twinspot,** *Hypargos niveoguttatus.*
5½ in. The female yellowish-brown instead of red, with grey cheeks.
East Africa.

meat, all mixed with ground hemp and a little grated carrot to make it moist. Whenever possible, this mixture should include fresh ants' eggs. In addition, the wren must have insects, either freshly killed or, preferably, alive. Wrens quarrel amongst each other and must therefore be kept apart outside the breeding season. They occasionally breed in a bird-room. Male and female are accustomed to each other like robins (p. 79).

Occasionally, we find woodpeckers in captivity. Both the greater spotted woodpecker and the lesser spotted woodpecker have a lively and cheerful disposition and become very tame. In their natural surroundings, they climb vertically along tree trunks with the help of their tail. They will therefore need a special cage. The cage for the greater spotted woodpecker must be at least 5 ft. high, 5 ft. long and 20 in. wide. Back and sides are lined with split fir branches to give the birds an opportunity to climb. The lesser spotted woodpecker can be put into a smaller cage, measuring 40 in. × 40 in. × 20 in. The young are fed on fresh, and soaked, ants' eggs, cream cheese, finely minced meat and egg-loaf. Later, they should be fed on a soft mixture. They should also have hemp, sunflower seed, etc., hazel nuts and a few mealworms. Woodpeckers are quarrelsome in cages, especially amongst each other, although a single bird of the small variety will usually get on well with the other inmates of

Woodpecker cage, lined with split sticks.
Below: horizontal section

the bird-room. The greater spotted woodpecker is not only aggressive towards other members of his race, but will be a danger to any bird. Lesser spotted woodpeckers can sometimes be kept in pairs in large outdoor aviaries.

The wryneck belongs to the same family, but does not climb trees and can therefore be accommodated in the same type of cage—provided it is at least 32 in. long—as the song-birds. The young are hand reared, the adult birds are fed like wood-peckers, except that fully grown wrynecks have no seed, but should have plenty of fresh ants' eggs during the summer.

The cuckoo needs a very spacious cage, at least 4 ft. long, 2 ft. high and 16 in. wide. Occasionally, we find a song-bird's nest in the garden which includes a cuckoo hatched from an egg laid there by its mother. At first, give it the same food as nightingales have: fresh ants' eggs and live insects, and later a mixture of finely chopped hard-boiled egg, scraped meat, fresh—in winter, dried—ants' eggs, cream cheese and meal-worms, with as many live insects as possible. Great care must be taken during the migrating season, because cuckoos travel at night and can hurt themselves badly against the bars of the cage if they are completely in the dark. Therefore install a very weak light, which must not, however, disturb the sleep of the other birds. The cuckoo should not be kept with smaller birds. He is best put into a cage of his own, but is a lazy and dirty bird and is not really worth troubling about.

There is indeed great variety amongst the soft-bills. Some will settle down well in captivity, some less so. But many true bird-lovers will feel, with William Blake, that 'a robin red-breast in a cage puts all the heavens in a rage'. Undoubtedly, birds are enjoyed more in freedom and we must be glad that they are protected by law.

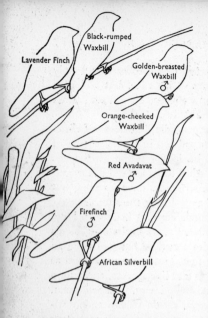

Lavender Finch

Black-rumped Waxbill

Golden-breasted Waxbill ♂

Orange-cheeked Waxbill

Red Avadavat ♂

Firefinch ♂

African Silverbill

Black-rumped Waxbill, *Estrilda troglodytes.* 3¾ in. Africa, from Senegal to northern Abyssinia, and Red Sea. The very similar Waxbill, *Estrilda astrild* lives further south (as far as the Cape) and is distinctly barred on the back. The Crimson-rumped Waxbill, *Estrilda rhodopyga* from north-east Africa, has red wing and tail coverts. **Lavender Finch,** *Estrilda caerulescens.* 4¼ in. West Africa. **Golden-breasted Waxbill,** *Amandava subflave,* also called *Estrilda s.* 3¾ in. The female without the red eye streak, and generally much paler. Africa, south of the Sahara. **Orange-cheeked Waxbill,** *Estrilda melpoda.* 4 in. West and central Africa. **Red Avadavat,** *Amandava amandava.* 3¾ in. Female and male in non-breeding dress greyish-brown above, and lighter below. Wings and flanks dotted with white, rump orange. Southern India to southern China and Java. Several varieties. **Firefinch,** *Estrilda senegala,* also known as *Lagonosticta s.* 4 in. The female brown above, lighter yellowish-brown below, rump red. Africa, from the edge of the Sahara to Natal. Many varieties. **African Silverbill,** *Euodice cantans.* 4½ in. Africa, from Senegal to East Africa and Red Sea coast. The very similar Indian Silverbill, *Euodice malabarica,* has a white rump and white tail coverts. It occurs throughout India and Afghanistan.

Red-throated Parrot Finch, *Erythrura psittacea.* 5¼ in. The female less brilliant. New Caledonia. **Long-tailed Munia,** *Erythrura prasina.* 6 in. The female duller, without blue markings, and with ochre underparts. Southern India to Indonesia. The Blue-faced Parrot Finch, *Erythrura trichroa,* a native of northern Australia, has a short tail. **Gouldian Finch,** *Chloebia gouldiae.* 5¼ in. Both the Red- and the Black-headed variety occur throughout northern Australia. All colours somewhat paler in the female. **Java Sparrow,** *Padda oryzivora.* 6½ in. Formerly only in Java and Bali, but the descendants of imported birds have spread beyond south-east Asia, as far as East Africa and St. Helena. **Diamond Sparrow,** *Staganopleura guttata,* also called *Steganopleura g.* 4½ in. South-eastern Australia. **Bicheno Finch,** *Stizoptera bichenovii,* also called *Stictoptera b.* 4 in. Eastern and northern Australia. Several varieties.

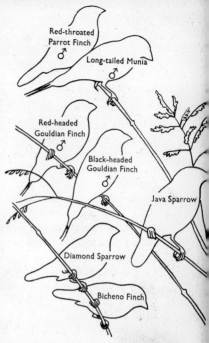

There is an almost infinite variety of tropical birds to choose from. Some are fairly hardy and not very difficult to feed. But, unless specifically mentioned otherwise, most of them will have to be kept in a warm room during the winter.

First, the birds that present no great problem in regard to feeding and accommodation. The grackles, from south-east Asia, have attractive voices. Some of them even learn a few words, many can whistle tunes or will imitate the song of other birds; they usually become very tame and are devoted to their keepers. Grackles occur in great variety, and can be identified by the shape and size of the yellow skin patch on the head. They need spacious individual cages—at least four times their own length—and are fed like thrushes, with the addition of a little meat, cream cheese, mealworms, insects, green stuff and, most important of all, fresh fruit and berries.

This also applies to Australian magpies, which are discussed at greater length in the chapter on crows (p. 188). Australian magpies, too, have good voices. A cage for a single bird should be at least 52 in. long. They are given a thrush mixture, boiled rice and chopped boiled potatoes, soaked bread, raw chopped meat, cream cheese and fruit, flavoured with a dried insect mixture.

Asian starlings and mynas and African glossy starlings can be kept in a flight-cage, a bird-room, or—in summer—in an aviary, but care must be taken to prevent birds of the same species from pairing, because they would then, in all probability, attack other inhabitants of the aviary and might injure them very badly. Although foreign starlings may last for many years in individual cages, they cannot display their characteristic vitality and agility in such confined space. It is therefore better to keep one pair of this group, or an assortment, consisting of one bird of each variety, in an enclosure. If they must be kept in cages, these should not be less than 32 in. long for single birds of the larger breeds, and at least 28 in. long for those of the smaller kinds. Mynas and foreign starlings should also be given a thrush mixture, consisting of two parts grated carrot, or apple, and one part each of dried ants' eggs, maggots, cream cheese and ground hemp, with finely minced raw meat; another mixture consists of white bread, soaked in milk or water, dried ants' eggs, raw scraped meat and soaked, dried berries. This is supplemented by live insects, mealworms, and fruit of every kind, and, if possible, seeds such as millet and hemp, and green food.

The smaller Asian starlings, amongst them the brahminy myna and the grey-headed myna, will sometimes breed in large flight-cages or aviaries. The young are given the same food as their parents, but need rather more live insects. The mynas from south-east Asia and from the Tropics are hardier, and are also good singers. They, too, will breed in captivity. The common myna and the bank myna are frequently imported.

The African glossy starlings have a metallic sheen, sometimes even a brilliant plumage. They occur in great variety and are frequently long lived. A purple glossy starling in the Berlin Zoo was well over thirty years old. The splendid glossy starling is a metallic bluish-green. One of the most handsome in this group is the superb starling, surpassed only in looks by the golden-breasted starling. Glossy starlings breed in hollows, like all other starlings and mynas, and must therefore have starling boxes in their aviaries. The rather long-tailed yellow-breasted starling needs a bigger cage than his humbler relations, who can be accommodated like mynas and Asian starlings.

Other starlings come from America, amongst them the attractive hangnests. The military starling, rice bird and bay-winged cowbird like to be close to the ground and therefore need a comparatively large area. The thick-billed varieties—the starlings proper—like seeds, both ripe and unripe. They are otherwise given the same food as the Asian starlings, but it must be remembered that the hangnests are rather delicate. Feed them with the usual thrush mixture, improving it with finely minced, lean raw meat, egg-loaf, ants, and maggots—these should be as fresh as possible—as great a variety of fresh fruit as can be provided, and live insects, but omitting seed. Starlings are often aggressive towards smaller birds and can even be a danger to them. Kept with larger birds, they will enliven any aviary or bird-room. They spend a lot of time on the ground and thus fill space that would frequently remain unused. Many varieties, amongst them the military starling, even sleep on the ground. American starlings need the same type of single cage as Asian or African starlings of the equivalent size. Hangnests do not nest on the ground, but in nests, which can be elaborate structures. The bay-winged cowbird rears its own young; other members of the species *molothrus* are parasitic, like the cuckoo, and lay their eggs in the nests of other birds.

Military starlings, rice birds and bay-winged cowbirds are frequently imported; red-winged blackbirds hardly at all. Hangnests appear regularly in pet shops. Their attractive colour and pleasant disposition—they are far less quarrelsome than other related birds—make them highly suitable for aviaries and flight-cages. The Brazilian hangnest—by no means unique in this respect—is also a good singer.

There are, unfortunately, very few opportunities to keep a bird of paradise. The principal home of these birds is New Guinea, although several varieties occur in Australia and on the Moluccas. They are fairly common, but are strictly protected and therefore almost unobtainable. Over thirty species have been kept in captivity in the past. Most birds of paradise present no special problems. They need large cages. Birds of starling size have cages at least 48 in. long, 20 in. wide and 24 in. high; larger birds belong in the aviary or bird-room. The greater bird of paradise is occasionally offered for sale. Like its lesser brethren, it is given a thrush mixture, improved with boiled rice, semolina, chopped boiled carrots, finely chopped hard-boiled egg and as much fruit as possible, with some green food. Provided they have enough space, birds of paradise are lively and agile. The male will even perform his display dance. Some specimens have lived in captivity for many years.

The calandra lark stands out amongst other foreign larks by virtue of its song, which far surpasses that of the skylark. A calandra lark will even mock the voice of other birds. It needs a 32-in. long lark cage and should have the same food as a skylark.

The Chinese jay thrush and the white-crested thrush have little in common with our jays, except the noise they make when they encounter anything likely to upset them. Their closest relative is the black-headed sibia. Chinese and white-crested jay thrushes come from the warmer regions of Asia. Being lively, strong, and fond of moving in jumps, they need ample space. A cage for a single bird should be 40 in. long, 16 in. wide and 24 in. high, and the birds can be kept in outdoor aviaries. Feed them on a thrush mixture in addition to scraped lean meat, insects, fruit, berries and green food. A single white-crested jay thrush is best kept in a cage of its own. A pair can be kept in an outdoor aviary, where they can be safely left during the winter, provided there is some shelter from draughts. The Chinese jay thrush, too, is not sensitive to cold.

There are many kinds of mocking-birds; they all come from the New World. Some are excellent singers, but this varies greatly, even amongst birds of the same species. Many mocking-birds imitate the song of other birds, which can make their own song more interesting or almost unbearable. It is entirely a question of luck whether our particular mocking-bird will please or annoy us. Mocking-birds are fed like our native thrushes. They need a very nourishing mixture and as many fresh ants' eggs as possible, some chopped egg, egg-loaf, and live insects, berries and fruit. The North American mocking-bird is the best-known representative of its group. Its qualities as a singer have been much debated, because the performances of individual birds differ so much. If they are kept for their song, mocking-birds should have separate cages, advisable in any case, because they are also rather quarrelsome. Mocking-birds breed readily in a spacious aviary. Their nests are built in shrubs. The young are reared on live insects, ants' eggs and mealworms. Remember, in particular, that mocking-birds are very sensitive to cold.

The babblers from southern Asia have always been much in demand. The red-billed liothrix—also called the Pekin robin

—is kept in a cage of its own, which should not be less than 24 in. long. The larger silver-eared mesia needs a slightly bigger cage—28 in. long—the smaller blue-winged siva can be put in the same type of cage as the red-billed liothrix. All three can be fed on a branded soft mixture. In summer, supplement this with a few fresh ants' eggs, fresh fruit and berries. These, of course, should also be added in winter, when ants' eggs can be replaced with mealworms. The red-billed liothrix sings very pleasantly, but is apt to disturb the other inhabitants of the bird-room by its restlessness. If a single pair is kept in an outdoor aviary, the birds will probably breed. The silver-eared mesia, though very pretty, is not a good singer, in contrast to the less conspicuous blue-winged siva, which can generally be safely kept in the bird-room. Blue-winged sivas have bred in captivity in the past. The three last-named birds need the same type of food, mixed with fresh ants' eggs, egg-loaf, sultanas and cut-up mealworms for rearing the young.

The black-headed sibia, a skilful climber and a poor singer, comes from the southern slopes of the Himalayas. Its cage should be at least 48 in. long. It is given the same food as other babblers. Pairs can be kept in outdoor aviaries during the summer.

The scimitar babblers occur in an area extending from Australia to south-east Asia, and resemble the jay thrushes in their habits. They are treated similarly, but it must be realised that they are sensitive to cold. Being rather quarrelsome, they should not be kept with other birds. Amongst the most frequently imported varieties is Hartort's scimitar babbler.

Southern Asia is the home of many other thrushes, some of them gaily coloured. They should be kept in cages of their own, because they are very aggressive. One of the most beautiful birds amongst them—and also one of the finest singers—is the common shama. Its cage should be 30 in. long, 20 in. wide and 20 in. high. It is fed like a nightingale, with as many ants' eggs as possible. In summer, these should be fresh. Mealworms, small berries, chopped fruit and chopped sultanas must always be added; a little finely minced meat and finely chopped hard-boiled egg is given occasionally. The common shama has often bred in captivity, even in spacious flight-cages, although it is most likely to nest in the shrubs of an aviary. The female takes from 12 to 13 days to hatch the eggs; the young stay in their nests for about the same span. The nest can be built in the fork of a branch, on an extra support, or in starling boxes. When the parent birds are feeding their young, they need as many live insects as possible, fresh ants' eggs, cockroaches, and some earth, which the shama needs in common with other thrushes. The magpie (or Straits robin)—fed and accommodated like the common shama—does not sing quite as well as the latter, but has, nevertheless, a pleasant voice. The slightly larger grey-and-orange ground thrush is quite an exceptional singer. The plumbeous thrush, from Cuba and the West Indies, and the grey-and-orange ground thrush both need a slightly bigger cage—not less than from 32 to 34 in. long—than the shama. They are fed like our native thrushes.

The graceful white-eyes occur throughout the warmer regions of Asia, Australia, New Zealand and Africa. They are very agile and love to skip about. Despite their small size, they need a comparatively large cage—at least 24 in. long—which, however, will hold a pair. They are given a good soft mixture, or a mixture of dried ants' eggs, egg-loaf, and grated apple or carrot, with a little chopped hard-boiled egg and cream cheese, fruit and berries, fresh ants' eggs, and as many live insects as possible. White-eyes are quite peaceful in bird-rooms and aviaries, but cannot always be fed properly there. They soon grow tame and friendly and have a pleasant, though not very loud, song. They are frequently offered for sale, especially the Indian variety shown in the illustration.

The bulbuls also inhabit the tropical and sub-tropical zone of Africa and Asia. They are given the same soft mixture as the shama and the magpie robin, with the addition of fruit and berries, of which they are very fond. They should also have mealworms regularly. Single birds or pairs should have cages of their own, because they frequently quarrel if they are kept with other birds, or even with large numbers of their own kind. Some bulbuls are good singers, and quite a few are also attractively coloured. The cage for a red-whiskered bulbul

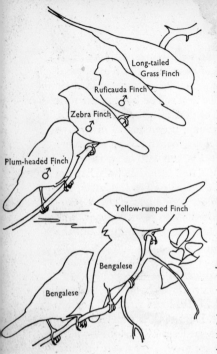

Long-tailed Grass Finch, *Poëphila acuticauda.* 7 in. Northern Australia. There is also a Red-billed variety. **Ruficauda Finch,** *Neochmia ruficauda.* 4¼ in. The female with less red on face, lighter and duller below. Northern and north-eastern Australia. **Zebra Finch,** *Taeniopygia guttata,* also called *T. castanotis.* 4¼ in. The female without brown ear patch and without markings on throat and breast. Australia. **Plum-headed Finch,** *Aidemosyna modesta.* 4½ in. The female has less red on the crown. Eastern Australia. **Yellow-rumped Finch,** *Lonchura flaviprymna,* also called *Munia f.* 4½ in. North-western and northern Australia. **Bengalese.** Not a wild species, but probably bred by the Japanese. It occurs in a variety of colours and is probably descended from the Sharp-tailed Munia, *Lonchura striata.* 4¾ in. Throughout southern China and Formosa, southern India and south-east Asia, as far as Indonesia.

---

should be at least 28 in. long; for the white-cheeked and the golden-vented bulbul not less than 32 in., and for pairs correspondingly longer.

The members of the genus *Chloropsis,* known in Britain as fruitsuckers—there is no proper English name for them, although they are sometimes mistakenly called green bulbuls—from south-east Asia, are all brightly coloured. They depend on fruit even more than bulbuls and should therefore be given chopped apples, pears, peaches, oranges, tangerines, bananas, figs, dates, sultanas and as great a variety of berries as possible. Depending on size, these fruits are cut up or given whole. Oranges and tangerines are cut in half, so that the birds can get at the juice. In addition, give them a standard nightingale

Tri-coloured Nun, *Lonchura malacca.* 4½ in. From southern India to southern China, Java, Sumatra, Philippines. Many varieties, amongst them the **Black-headed Nun,** *Lonchura atricapilla,* which occurs chiefly in India and Indo-China. The White-headed Nun, *Lonchura maja,* differs little from the Black-headed Nun, except for its white head and throat. Malay Peninsula. **Two-coloured Manikin,** *Spermestes bicolor.* 3¾ in. Cameroons to Somaliland, Abyssinia to Natal. Many varieties; the bird in the illustration, with brown back and shoulders, comes from West Africa. **Magpie Manikin,** *Spermestes fringilloides.* 4½ in. Tropical Africa, as far as Natal. **Chestnut-breasted Finch,** *Lonchura castaneothorax.* 4½ in. Northern and eastern Australia, several varieties. The White-breasted Finch, *Lonchura pectoralis,* from northern Australia has a band of white-tipped black feathers, instead of the brown patch, on the breast; otherwise a pale vinaceous brown below and a brownish silver-grey above. **Spotted Munia,** *Lonchura punctulata.* 4¾ in. From Ceylon and southern India to southern China, Formosa, Malay Peninsula and Philippines.

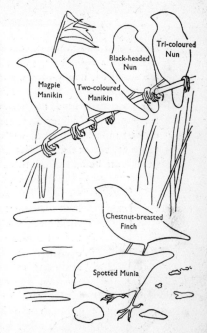

Magpie Manikin

Two-coloured Manikin

Black-headed Nun

Tri-coloured Nun

Chestnut-breasted Finch

Spotted Munia

---

mixture and live insects. Some birds of this group are good singers. They are kept in the same type of cage as the larger bulbuls. The species most frequently encountered in pet shops is the gold-fronted fruitsucker.

Male sunbirds are often brilliantly coloured. Some portions of their plumage are iridescent with a metallic sheen. In disposition, sunbirds resemble tits: like the latter they are always moving about and flitting from branch to branch. Most sunbirds come from Africa, but some varieties occur in the warmer parts of Asia and Australia. In freedom, sunbirds live on small insects, and on nectar, which they draw from blossoms with their beaks and tongues, exactly like the American humming-birds. As a substitute, give all nectar feeders—whether they are sunbirds, honey-eaters, sugar-birds or humming-birds—a mixture made up by dissolving three-quarters of a teaspoon of a good baby food, two teaspoonfuls of demerara sugar, two teaspoonfuls of honey and one teaspoonful of sweetened condensed milk in a pint of water. This liquid is then placed in tubes or, better still, special drinking pipes, which prevent the birds from being soaked. Such pipes can easily be made by any

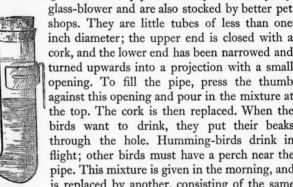

glass-blower and are also stocked by better pet shops. They are little tubes of less than one inch diameter; the upper end is closed with a cork, and the lower end has been narrowed and turned upwards into a projection with a small opening. To fill the pipe, press the thumb against this opening and pour in the mixture at the top. The cork is then replaced. When the birds want to drink, they put their beaks through the hole. Humming-birds drink in flight; other birds must have a perch near the pipe. This mixture is given in the morning, and is replaced by another, consisting of the same proportions of water, honey and demerara sugar, but without any baby food or condensed milk. Both mixtures must be freshly made every day.

Drinking pipe for humming-birds

In addition, nectar feeders must have many small live insects. To make sure that the birds can get their insects, keep them in glass-fronted cages, whose sides consist of finely meshed wire. If live insects are not available, the nectar substitute must be made more nourishing by beating a raw egg—both yolk and white—into it. Also, put fruit—apples, pears, or bananas—mealworms and ants' eggs into an electric mixer and add the result to the nectar mixture. It is most important that everything should be liquid and sweet.

The cage for a single sunbird must be at least 24 in. long, and a cage for a pair at least 40 in. long. All nectar feeders should be sprayed with tepid water every other day to keep their plumage in good condition, since they can become very dirty on their rather sticky diet. Use a flower spray for this purpose. If pot plants are put into the cage, the birds will bathe by moving to and fro between the damp leaves. Some sunbirds have a pleasant voice. The scarlet-chested sunbird occurs throughout Africa and is imported fairly frequently.

The sugarbirds from the South American tropics and the honey-eaters from Australia and the Pacific also need blossoms. The honey-eaters are less brilliantly coloured and are therefore not kept so often. Amongst the sugarbirds, by contrast, some really spectacular varieties are to be found, which are highly sought after. They are fed on the same nectar mixture as sunbirds. Sugarbirds also need a good soft mixture, or grated hard-boiled egg, mixed with grated egg-loaf, and, in addition, finely chopped figs, chopped bananas and pears, fresh ants' eggs and small mealworms. They also like other live insects. Sugarbirds appear at their best in glass-fronted cages; these should be of the same size and type as the cages for sunbirds. But while the latter must always be kept warm, sugarbirds are not quite so delicate, although they must never be exposed to cold and draughts. One of the best-looking members of this group is the yellow-winged sugarbird, who rather resembles the sunbirds in shape. The blue sugarbird is less spectacular, though still very attractive. It has a comparatively short beak.

Humming-birds are imported very rarely, although they will live many years, if they are given the right nectar mixture and insects. Even the smallest amongst them need ample space to fly about. A cage for two or three birds must be at least 40 in. long, 24 in. high, and 24 in. wide. Humming-birds always fly, never skip, and therefore only need one long perch, from which they set forth on their explorations. Always fill a cage with birds of different varieties, since members of the same breed usually quarrel. The birds can have pot plants, provided these do not affect their freedom of movement in the air. If the plants are sprayed, the birds will bathe in the leaves. Many humming-birds perform remarkable display flights and have clear, strong voices. The cages must be kept as warm as possible. The temperature of the room must never drop below 70 deg. F. (20 deg. C.).

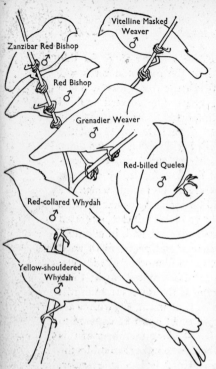

Zanzibar Red Bishop, *Euplectes nigroventris*. 4 in. Female and male in non-breeding dress similar to female of the larger Grenadier Weaver. East Africa. The **Red Bishop,** *Euplectes orix franziscana*. 4¾ in., occurs from West Africa to Somaliland, the **Grenadier Weaver,** *Euplectes orix orix*, 5¼ in., in East and South Africa. In both varieties, female and male in non-breeding dress are light brown, with darker patches above, and somewhat lighter—the breast with darker streaks—below and on the wing coverts. The very similar Black-winged Red Bishop, *Euplectes hordeacea*, 4½ in., comes from the grasslands of Africa. The male in breeding dress has a red forehead, a wide red band across the throat and dark brown wing coverts. **Red-billed Quelea,** *Quelea quelea*. 4¾ in. The female without any black and red, the head greyish-brown above with whitish throat. Africa, south of the Sahara. Many varieties. **Red-collared Whydah,** *Euplectes ardens*, also called *Coliuspasser a.* The male in breeding dress up to 26 in. (incl. tail), otherwise, like female, short-tailed; pale brown with dark patches above and lighter below. **Yellow-shouldered Whydah,** *Euplectes macrocercus*, also called *Coliuspasser macrocercus*. Male in breeding dress 11½ in. Female short-tailed, light brown above, brownish-white below, with buff flanks. Male in non-breeding dress like female, except for yellow shoulder patch. Africa, south of the Sahara, as far as Rhodesia. The White-winged Whydah, *Euplectes albonotatus*, also called *Coliuspasser a.*, is very similar, but has a white shoulder patch. **Vitelline Masked Weaver,** *Malimbus vitellinus*, also called *Ploceus v.* 5¼ in. Female and male in non-breeding dress, light brown with darker streaks above, pale yellow below. Cheeks and rump yellowish. West Africa to Nile. Several varieties.

Brazilian Hangnest, *Icterus jamaicaii.* 8 in. Northern South America to Paraguay. **Bay-winged Cowbird,** *Molothrus badius.* 7½ in. Bolivia to Argentine. **Rice Bird,** *Dolichonyx oryzivorus.* 6¾ in. The female yellowish olive brown above, streaked with black, and a light yellowish-olive below. North America. **Red-winged Blackbird** *Agelaius phoeniceus.* 9 in. The female blackish-brown above, streaked light brown, and buff-white, with darker patches, below. Wing coverts usually edged with red. North America. Several varieties. **Military Starling,** *Sturnella militaris.* 10 in. The female with less red. South America, Chile, Patagonia. Formerly, many other kinds of starlings and troupals used to be imported from the U.S.A., where they are now protected. Today, they are mostly caught in their winter quarters in central and South America.

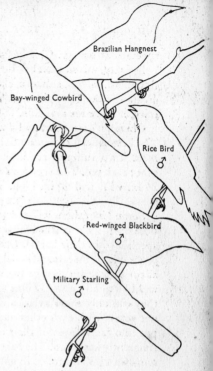

The pittas resemble thrushes in looks and behaviour, although they are not related to them. These short-tailed birds like to keep to the ground, where they can move very fast. Some varieties, such as the green-breasted pitta, are brilliantly coloured. Their cage must cover a minimum area of 40 × 40 in. and the bottom of the tray should be covered with a sponge rubber mat, which has to be frequently washed with hot water. Pittas are given a good soft mixture, to which raw meat, chopped into small pieces, is added. They should also have fresh ants' eggs, mealworms and other live insects, like grasshoppers, etc. Pittas have already bred in captivity in small, well-planted hot-houses. In cages, these tropical birds from Africa, Asia and Australia have to be kept singly.

Some of the chatterers from South America are of an almost

spectacular beauty. Chiefly fruit eaters, they should be given boiled rice, mixed with cut-up apples, pears, bananas, oranges, figs, dates, raisins, sultanas, chopped boiled carrots and a little cream cheese. They also need a little raw meat and bare young mice, if these are available.

Chatterers are quiet and do not like to move about too fast. The best-known representative of this group is the cock-of-the-rock. Two varieties are imported, one apricot-coloured, the other dark red. The cage for a single bird should be 48 in. long, 24 in. wide and 40 in. high. The smaller chatterers need less space.

Some kingfishers will not take too badly to captivity. This does not include the fish-eating varieties, which are too specialised in their habits. Others, such as kookaburras, which go after large insects and small reptiles in the manner of shrikes, adapt themselves to cage life very well. They have strong legs and like to hop about. Since they attack and eat smaller birds, they can only share aviaries with larger companions; they do not get on with each other and should, therefore, generally be put into large cages of their own. These Australian birds are frequently imported. They should be given raw meat—cut into narrow strips and rolled in ants' eggs or in an insect mixture—mice and small fishes. The cage must be at least 48 in. long, 24 in. wide and 40 in. high. The laughing kookaburra is fairly hardy, becomes very tame and makes itself heard quite often.

Exotic woodpeckers are only rarely imported. They are treated like our native breeds. The closely related barbets present few problems. Since they are not climbers, but hop from perch to perch, they will not require a special cage. Feed them with a good thrush mixture, and cut-up fruit and berries, mealworms, ants' eggs and raw meat; some prefer fruit to all other food. Barbets are also best put into individual cages, and these, in the case of the blue-throated barbet, from northern India, must be at least 40 in. long. Pairs need correspondingly more space. In summer, barbets can be put into an outdoor aviary, where they will need a minimum area of 5 to 7 sq. yd. per pair.

The South American toucans and aracaris are brightly

coloured and quickly grow tame. They, too, are fruit eaters. Give them a mixture of chopped fruit of all kinds, chopped boiled carrots, boiled rice and soaked bread, formed into small dumplings. Occasionally, add chopped raw meat or boiled egg. The birds take these dumplings into their bills, toss them into the air and then let them disappear quickly down their throats. They should also be given young mice and large insects from time to time. The cage for a single toucan must be at least 56 in. long, with a height and width of 24 in. The perches—two will be sufficient—must be very thick and strong. The smaller aracaris will be content with slightly less space. Toucans are usually kept on their own; if enough space is available, several varieties can be kept together, thus creating an attractive ensemble. The green-billed toucan, a typical representative of this group, is regularly imported; giant toucans are increasingly difficult to obtain.

The touracos and go-away birds are African fruit eaters of conspicuous beauty. They fly, skip, and run along branches with equal skill. Give them a thrush mixture and cut-up fruit of every kind, with boiled rice, grated carrot, finely chopped hard-boiled egg and chopped green food. They should also have live insects. Being fairly big and lively, they need a lot of space. They can share a large flight-cage or bird-room with other birds of a similar size. Several touracos of the same, or a related, variety generally live well together. The Knysna touraco, amongst others, is frequently offered for sale. Go-away birds and plantain eaters are less spectacular and therefore not so much in demand.

Many tropical members of the cuckoo family are easier to keep than our native breed. This applies especially to the magnificent coucals, birds that can run and hop with great speed and prefer to keep close to the ground. The Senegal coucal is regularly imported. It should be given a thrush mixture, cut-up raw meat, insects, young mice or even dead young sparrows. Its cage should resemble that of the toucan. It can share an aviary or bird-room with larger birds, such as touracos, or with the rather strong glossy starlings, but is quite unsafe with smaller birds.

Foreign seed-eaters have become increasingly popular during the last few years. Finches, especially, have found many enthusiasts, because some varieties are easy to keep and will breed readily. Others require considerable care and attention. Some of them, like the Java sparrow, the zebra finch and the bengalese have become real domestic pets. The beginner is apt to be confused by the great variety of names. But whether we call them astrilds, manikins, amadines, or whydahs, regardless of whether they are described as finches or not, they all belong to the same family and come from the tropical and sub-tropical regions of Africa, Asia and Australia. Their home is usually in steppes and grasslands, sometimes also in fields, forests and swamps. Their food consists chiefly of seeds and insects. But, however different they appear, their basic needs differ very little.

Exotic finches are sociable birds, although breeding pairs will often turn against members of their own or similar species. Therefore, only keep one pair of a particular variety in the bird-room, although it is perfectly safe to keep several breeding pairs in the same enclosure, provided they are different species. Finches should never be kept in single cages, because they become very miserable without company. Even a cage for a pair of the smallest varieties must be at least 20 in. long, 12 in. wide and 14 in. high. The bars must be no more than $\frac{3}{8}$ in. apart to prevent the birds from slipping through. A box-cage, with a wooden lid, will afford the best protection against draughts. It is also necessary to provide a sleeping place in the form of a nesting-box, which should be placed against an opening outside the cage. It can also be hung up in the cage itself, if there is enough room. The birds will frequently nest there, although they can be given a roller travelling-cage—where they will build little round nests with side entrances—or little wire baskets for this purpose. The young are hatched within 11 to 13 days, but it is quite some time before they leave the nest. When it is no longer needed, the old nest is removed and its wire frame or box is thoroughly cleaned with insecticide.

One breeding pair per cage, only a few birds for the flight-cage or aviary—this is the successful breeder's motto. If several pairs are kept together they must have ample space to avoid each other. Each pair should have at least two sleeping places and two nesting-boxes to avoid quarrels. Foreign finches can be put in an outdoor aviary during the summer, but here also overcrowding must be avoided and no more than one breeding pair allowed for an area of 3 sq. yd. Suitable breeding places can be provided in bird-rooms or large flight-cages by cutting off corners with wooden frames, stretched with wide-meshed wire-netting. This space is then filled with brushwood (ill. p. 41). The birds can get into the branches through the opening in the wire and can build their nests in complete seclusion. This arrangement also allows us to keep larger birds with breeding pairs. The finches must be brought indoors before the onset of frost, although acclimatised foreign finches are often quite hardy. Their winter quarters must be fairly light, so that the birds can see their food, even on dark days; otherwise it is necessary to provide artificial light. Perches and branches should be arranged in such a way that they can easily be kept clean. There must be enough feeding and drinking bowls for all, otherwise the weaker birds would be prevented from eating and drinking by the stronger inmates. Flat saucers, filled with water, provide an opportunity for bathing.

Quite often, finches—although apparently thriving—will not breed. This is often due to an unbalanced diet. In freedom, these birds live on unripe or sprouting seed, insects and green food. They need the same food in captivity. A seed mixture can be made up of various kinds of millet, canary seed, rye grass, clipped oats, a good siskin mixture and poppy seed. Provide, also, some spray millet, soaked—in winter, sprouting —millet, chickweed and other green food and, in summer, as great a variety of unripe seeds as possible, such as seeding grasses of all kinds.

During the breeding season, and when the birds are raising

their young, also give them ants' eggs, either fresh or dried and soaked in milk, cut-up mealworms, a good soft mixture, chopped hard-boiled egg, grated egg-loaf and rusks. Some birds refuse insects or only give them to their young for the first few days, if at all. The more the menu can be varied, the fitter the birds will be. The cuttlefish bone must never be missing, because it provides the birds with badly needed calcium. In aviaries with only a few inmates, some millet can even be sown. This is not possible amongst too many birds, where the plants would merely be receptacles for dirt. If the finches seem reluctant to hatch their eggs or are indifferent parents, use bengalese or zebra finches as foster-parents. Their own eggs must be taken away, in this case, since they would otherwise lose all interest in their charges as soon as these were able to leave the nest, and would devote themselves entirely to their own young.

When buying foreign finches, it is essential to remember that they usually arrive in great numbers and have often been kept in a very small space. It is therefore quite likely that one will get a sick bird. Newcomers must be isolated and given the best attention for this reason. They can only be allowed to join other birds when it is certain that they are not diseased.

Bengalese are hardy and long lived and have been bred in captivity in the Far East for years. They have been known for over 250 years in Japan, where they enjoy great popularity. There are a number of varieties, all probably descended from the sharp-tailed munia, a native of southern Asia. Breeding presents little difficulty. Some birds produce one brood after another during the summer. Pairs should be separated during the winter to prevent exhaustion and can be brought together again in spring.

The Java sparrow, too, is kept as a pet in Japan. It occurs in several colours, chiefly white, pied and 'natural', and is bred in large numbers. In Europe these large sturdy finches do not usually breed, although they are amongst the most rewarding cage-birds in every other respect.

Munias, also called nuns or manikins, are frequently seen in pet shops. Their home is southern Asia and Australia. The

most brightly coloured is the tri-coloured munia, which, unfortunately, is very delicate. Black- and white-headed munias,
by contrast, are hardy and will breed readily. The spotted
munia was amongst the earliest foreign finches to be imported;
its restrained colour is very attractive and it will breed without
difficulty. Yellow-rumped, chestnut-breasted and white-
breasted finches are more spectacularly coloured. They all
belong to the same group of Australian birds.

The manikins are also represented in Africa. The smaller
varieties will breed in cages. In a small space, breeding pairs are
rather aggressive towards other birds, and should therefore be
kept by themselves, unless they can be put into a fairly large
enclosure. The rufous-backed manikin and the closely related
black-and-white manikin—whose back and wings are black—
are considered much friendlier; the good nature of the magpie
manikin is almost proverbial.

Great numbers of African silverbills are regularly imported
from the grasslands of West and East Africa. They are distinguished from the otherwise similar Indian silverbills by their
dark rumps. The white-rumped Indian silverbill also appears
frequently in Europe. Both varieties are hardy and will breed
readily in cage and aviary. They are good singers and can
usually be bought for a small sum.

The cut-throat or ribbon finch, from Africa, is one of the
finest birds of its kind. It will nest in aviaries and bird-rooms.
Dr. Russ, the great German ornithologist, reported a pair
which had raised 176 young in three years. Cut-throats are apt
to disturb the broods of other finches if they are confined to a
fairly small area. They are less of a nuisance in the bird-room,
as long as it includes ample nesting facilities and is not over-
crowded. The South African red-headed finch is closely
related to the cut-throat.

The gaily coloured diamond sparrow from Australia will
breed without much difficulty in the bird-room, but is less
likely to do so in a cage. The painted finch is imported very
rarely, although it is quite common in its native Australia. It is
by no means easy to breed in captivity. The red-faced finch,
another Australian bird, will breed successfully, if a single pair

is put into a very spacious aviary. Its compatriot, the plum-headed finch, a bird of more restrained colour, may breed with some luck. Everything depends on not disturbing the parents while they are guarding the nest. The zebra finch occurs throughout Australia, where the breeding of new colours has been developed into a science of its own. Having first produced white, cinnamon and chestnut birds, breeders have now gone further and have created many different coloured sorts. Zebra finches will readily breed in cages; the young are hatched within eleven days and can fly after two and a half weeks. They are separated from their parents—like the young of all other foreign finches—as soon as they are independent, so as not to disturb further broods. Pairs must not be allowed to breed more than three or four times a year, because the birds would otherwise become exhausted.

Bicheno finches, also from Australia, are inconspicuously coloured, but strikingly patterned. They need a lot of insects, a soft mixture and unripened seeds, if they are to thrive in captivity. They build free-standing spherical nests with small entry-holes.

Two varieties of the long-tailed grass finch reach Europe regularly: the yellow-billed kind, and another, with a red bill, named after the famous zoologist, Ludwig Heck (*Poephila hecki*). The closely related black-tailed finch (*Poephila atropygialis*) has a short tail and black bill, while the masked finch (*Peophila personata*) is brown at the top of its head and at the nape and has a black mask. Grass finches frequently breed in flight-cages and aviaries. Masked finches are best kept in pairs in large cages; it is also advisable to separate them from other birds, if they are to breed.

The finest of all foreign finches is the gouldian finch, named after the great nineteenth-century ornithologist John Gould, who began life as a gardener and who, over a period of more than sixty years, compiled a large number of beautifully illustrated books. He travelled all over the world when to do so was still a far more dangerous undertaking than it is to-day. Many birds have been named after him. His books are now almost priceless treasures, carefully guarded by their fortunate owners.

There are three variants of the gouldian finch, one with a red head, one with a black head, and one with a yellow head. They inhabit the same part of northern Australia and are found in the same flock. Gouldian finches travel very badly. Considerable losses must therefore be reckoned with amongst newly imported birds. Once acclimatised, however, they are quite long lived. It is therefore best to get birds bred in captivity in England.

In this respect, gouldian finches resemble red-headed parrot finches, from south-east Asia to northern Australia and Samoa. They, too, travel very badly—probably because of the unbalanced diet on the journey—and are frequently in very poor condition on arrival, although they present few problems once they have fully recovered. Red-headed finches, like gouldian finches, will breed readily, especially if they are given a lot of green food. The nonpareil pintail, or long-tailed munia, is not unlike a tri-coloured or blue-headed parrot finch, except that it is yellow below, instead of green, and has a very much longer tail.

Avadavat and golden-breasted waxbills are amongst the smallest birds of their group. The avadavat comes from southern Asia, the golden-breasted waxbill from Africa. Both will breed readily and are fairly long lived. Eight- or ten-year-old birds are not rarities.

The quail finch and bar-breasted weaver finch are ground birds. They run about a great deal and therefore need a large area. Like all ground birds, they should not share cages with other birds, by whose droppings they would get badly soiled. Both varieties come from the African grasslands, the darkheaded bar-breasted weaver finch from West Africa, and the quail finch, whose head has white markings, from South Africa. Only one pair of each kind can be kept in the same enclosure during the breeding season, when these birds are rather aggressive towards other members of their breed. A single pair will do best in a bird-room, where it should be provided with a few hide-outs for nesting by putting down well-grown grass turves with slight gaps between them.

Another African bird, the green-winged pytilia, appears

regularly, but rather infrequently, on the market. It is very difficult to get this comparatively large finch to breed. It happens occasionally in a bird-room or in a well-planted outdoor aviary. The red-winged pytilia from the grasslands south of the Sahara has a calm and peaceful disposition. It also breeds very rarely in captivity and should not be encouraged to do so, except, possibly, in an aviary. Peter's twinspot, from East Africa, is attractively marked, neither shy nor quarrelsome, and therefore makes an ideal addition to flight-cage or bird-room, although it may occasionally attack kindred birds during the nesting period.

The African firefinches present few problems. The best-known variety is the firefinch from East Africa; like other birds of its kind, it will readily build a nest in captivity.

Some African waxbills have proved rewarding charges. Amongst them is the black-rumped waxbill, which can be highly recommended for beginners, despite its not very striking appearance. It makes no special demands and breeds without difficulty. Incubation lasts eleven days; the young are able to leave their nests after a fortnight. The crimson-rumped waxbill and common waxbill resemble the black-rumped waxbill. The first can be distinguished by its red rump, the second has a longer tail and brown markings below. The orange-cheeked waxbill is very common in captivity, but will rarely breed successfully, because the smallest disturbance is apt to drive it away from its nest, which is spherical with a covered side entrance. The lavender finch is quite outstandingly pretty. Unfortunately, it travels very badly and frequently arrives in poor condition. Once acclimatised, it is quite long lived, if it gets as many insects as possible. It does not, as a rule, breed in captivity. No more than one pair should be kept per aviary, since cocks are very aggressive towards each other.

The most beautiful of all African waxbills is the violet-eared waxbill. Although it will breed in captivity, the young have in the past only survived on rare occasions. Several varieties of cordon bleu are regularly imported. The males of the West African breeds have red cheek patches, which are absent in South African birds. They readily breed in large flight-cages and bird-rooms, but are not likely to do so in cramped surroundings.

To be successful as a breeder of tropical finches, one must learn to distinguish between males and females, even amongst breeds—such as the black-rumped waxbill, usually called the red-eared waxbill—in which both sexes have the same colouring. This is all the more difficult when the females also sing. Persistent observation is the only method, because the males will sooner or later perform their display dances. If the young are to be reared successfully, the prospective parents must get used to the rearing diet already before breeding. They will otherwise feed their young almost exclusively on ripe seeds, which do not suit them at all. Ripe seeds must therefore be cut down at an early stage, and replaced with green food and, especially, sprouting seeds. The chicks of many foreign finches present a fascinating picture with their bills wide open. The inside of the mandibles of each kind of bird is marked differently, often in brilliant colours.

The whydahs, or widows, from the African grasslands, are interesting, although rather difficult birds. They do not rear their own young, but lay their eggs in the nests of other birds—mostly finches—in the manner of the cuckoo. These eggs are hatched by the foster-parents, who rear the young with their own offspring. So far, very little has been discovered about the specific breeds chosen as foster-parents. Whydahs are housed and fed like tropical finches. The long-tailed varieties need comparatively large cages. If at all possible, they should be kept in a bird-room. A cage for a single whydah must be at least 48 in. long, 20 in. wide and 24 in. high. Breeding should only be encouraged in bird-rooms or aviaries. There is one great drawback to whydahs, however splendid they may look at times: the male wears his breeding dress (the male alone is long tailed) only for a very short period and resembles the female for the rest of the year. Pairs are therefore difficult to obtain. The apparent female often proves to be a male in non-breeding dress. The females of different breeds are not easy to tell apart. Breeding these magnificent birds is thus nearly impossible, for a number of reasons: lack of space, the difficulty in getting pairs and the absence of suitable foster-parents, who, in any case, would always have to be breeding at the same time as the whydahs. Even if all those problems could be solved, it would still be very doubtful whether the forcibly adopted parents would rear the young. In addition, male whydahs are very quarrelsome and can wreak havoc amongst each other in a confined space. A paradise whydah was bred in England in 1957.

The least spectacular representative of this group is the combassou or steel finch. The short-tailed male is an attractive bluish-black. These birds can be kept in spacious cages, where, however, they are apt to disturb other finches; the males also get on very badly amongst each other. They flutter around wildly, attacking every imaginary enemy. The combassou occasionally hatches its own eggs, although these are mostly laid in the nests of firefinches and common waxbills, and occasionally in those of smaller soft-bills. The young, in this case, will be reared entirely on insects by their foster-parents. The male of the shaft-tailed or queen whydah has four long feathers in its tail. These are completely bare, except for the ends. The young of this bird are probably brought up by violet-eared waxbills, in whose nests the eggs have been laid. The paradise whydah, with its long tail, is amongst the most attractive birds of its kind. Several varieties—which differ very little—are imported. Since the tail feathers of the male can be as much as 14 in. long, paradise whydahs need ample space. Their young are usually reared by the green-winged pytilia or by the less frequently kept Melba waxbill.

Several birds commonly described as whydahs—amongst them the white-winged widow bird, the red-collared widow bird and the yellow-shouldered widow bird—really belong to the weaver family (as do our house-sparrows). Like the weavers, widow birds build elaborate nests and rear their own young. Widow birds and weavers are quite easy to keep, but need a lot of space. Many varieties are polygamous. One male may pair with several females, either simultaneously or in quick succession. The male in non-breeding dress resembles the female. Since non-breeding dress is worn for quite some time, it is often very difficult to discover the sex of the newly acquired bird. This, of course, complicates breeding even further. Widow birds should be kept in large aviaries, preferably each kind by itself, and each male should have several females; the birds may, perhaps, breed under such conditions. Only the smaller varieties can share in flight-cages or aviaries with other birds, because the males of the weavers are always building nests and in this constructive pursuit frequently demolish every nest within reach for building materials. It is understandable that weavers—despite their good looks and the ease with which they can be obtained—have comparatively few friends amongst bird-keepers. One must specialise in them, if one wants to breed, and go to experienced dealers to make sure that females are obtained and not merely males in non-breeding dress. Finally, weavers need ample space. Yet many a bird-lover might find them well worth keeping, not least because there is still so much to be discovered about their breeding habits.

Widow birds and weavers are given the same mixture as tropical finches; apart from the two kinds of millet, Indian and white, they must have a good siskin mixture from time to time, as well as a soft mixture, live insects, fruit, a lot of green food, and sprouting, soaked and half-ripened seeds of every kind. Supplies of coconut fibre and grass stalks will enable the birds to make their nests. Frost must be carefully guarded against, although weavers are not particularly delicate.

It is, unfortunately, impossible to list more than a few varieties out of a large number. Size rules out Jackson's widow bird, with its 16 in. tail, for most bird-keepers. Other more frequently imported species are the yellow-shouldered widow bird and the red-collared widow bird, both with not too long tails. The closely related smaller weavers are often very prettily coloured. The males are usually red, golden-red or yellow-and-black. Red bishop and grenadier are frequently imported. Both are hardy and long lived and need some sort of thicket—through which they can creep—to build their nest in. The Zanzibar red bishop is not found in pet shops quite so often. The red-billed quelea from the African grasslands is cheap and comes to us in large quantities. Most of the birds offered for sale are, unfortunately, males who will build continuously throughout the year with great enthusiasm. Red-billed queleas have occasionally bred in captivity. Finally, it is necessary to single out the yellow weaver from this large group of birds, whose members are mostly distributed throughout Africa. Only very few weavers come from south-east Asia. The yellow weaver has on occasions bred in captivity. It is indeed most rewarding to observe these lively, skilful birds. A great deal is still to be discovered about them and they should be given every opportunity to breed.

Sparrows, as already mentioned, also belong to the weavers. Our native house- and tree-sparrows have already been discussed (p. 65). Their foreign relations are similarly fed and housed. Unsuitable for smaller cages, they will thrive in large flight-cages, aviaries and bird-rooms, where they will breed without difficulty. They build their nests in roller travelling-cages or in nesting-boxes. When rearing their young, they should be given a soft mixture, egg-loaf, chopped hard-boiled egg and ants' eggs. The Sudan golden sparrow from East Africa is frequently offered for sale; the golden sparrow, from Arabia, is more difficult to obtain.

The large family of the finches proper includes the rather attractive American siskins. They have the same requirements as their European cousins, except that they also need some soft food. Their seed mixture is always supplemented with millet; they should also be frequently given dandelion heads, thistle seed, alder and birch seed, etc. Siskins, unfortunately, often get a very unbalanced diet on the journey and therefore arrive in poor condition. The most handsome of all American siskins, the red hooded siskin, is frequently crossed with canaries. The American goldfinch is a lively creature of bright plumage. Several other siskins of this group, such as the sombre Magellan finch, the Arkansas goldfinch and the delightful Yarrel's siskin set no problems in bird-room or aviary and will also breed in larger enclosures. All Central and South American varieties must be protected from frost in winter.

The serin has many relations on the African continent. Some of them are good singers, others are attractively coloured. A cage for a single bird should be at least 20 in. long. Pairs need correspondingly larger accommodation—a cage with a minimum length of 30 in.—and must be isolated from their own kind and from other finches during the breeding season, when the males are most aggressive. Serins are happiest in a large outdoor aviary. They are given a mixture of Indian and white millet and, in addition, a siskin mixture, a lot of green food, and, occasionally, a soft mixture, mealworms and ants' eggs. When rearing their young, they also need soaked and unripe seeds, ants' eggs, egg-loaf and chopped hard-boiled egg. The incubating period lasts thirteen days, the young leave their nest 21 days after hatching. The grey canary or grey singing finch is chiefly kept for its song. The yellow-fronted canary, or green singing finch, is of a brighter hue and is also a good singer. Both have bred in captivity, not only in aviaries, but also in spacious cages.

The Far East is the home of a relative of our native hawfinch, the masked hawfinch, or masked grosbeak. It is a hardy and long-lived bird with an attractive song. Feed it like the European variety, adding twigs with fresh buds, green food and a few mealworms, with extra mealworms and ants' eggs when the young are reared. It will breed in outdoor aviaries, as will other foreign grosbeaks, which are occasionally offered for sale. Their nests are always built in shrubs.

The small finches of the genus *Sporophilia* are natives of America. They are long lived, can be kept in cage, birdroom or aviary, and frequently breed in captivity. They are fed like foreign finches, including the same extras when rearing their young. Having paired, they are usually aggressive towards other birds of the same or a related species, and must therefore be segregated if they are to breed. They do not, however, object to birds of other groups. Their nests are built in shrubs. Amongst the more frequently imported varieties, the guttural finch and the white-throated finch are highly recommended.

The Cuban finch and the olive finch are very prettily marked; they are good, though not very loud, singers. The Cuban finch has bred in captivity quite often, the olive finch very rarely.

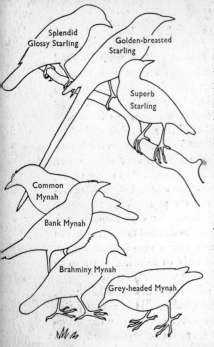

Splendid Glossy Starling, *Lamprotornis splendidus*, also called *Lamprocolius splendidus*. 10 in. West and Central Africa. The very similar Bronze-tailed Starling, *Lamprocolius chalcurus*, has a golden—instead of a pale yellow—iris; the Long-tailed Glossy Starling, which measures up to 20 in. resembles both, except for its long tail. **Golden-breasted Starling,** *Lamprotornis regius*, also called *Cosmopsarus r.* 14 in. East Africa. **Superb Starling,** *Lamprotornis superbus*, also called Spreo. 8½ in. East Africa. **Common Mynah,** *Sturnus tristis*, also called *Acridotheres t.* 8½ in. Afghanistan to Indo-China and Thailand. **Bank Mynah,** *Sturnus ginginianus*, also called *Acridotheres g.* 8½ in. Afghanistan, northern India. The Chinese Crested Mynah, *Sturnus cristatellus*, also called *Acridotheres c.* 10¾ in., China and Indo-China, is black above, dark grey below, and has a crest, but no bare patch behind the eye. **Brahminy Mynah,** *Sturnus pagodarum*, also called *Temenuchus p.* 8 in. Afghanistan, India, Ceylon. Several varieties. **Grey-headed Mynah,** *Sturnus malabaricus*, also called *Sturnia malabarica.* 7½ in. India. Several varieties.

Both are fed like other foreign finches and need a cage of 24 in. length per pair. They build their nests round wire baskets or in roller travelling-cages. Breeding is more likely to succeed in a less confined space; only one pair of either variety can be kept in an aviary, bird-room or flight-cage, since the males will immediately fight amongst each other. The young are reared on the same food as other foreign finches.

The crested finches are lively, cheerful birds and have a peaceful disposition outside the breeding season. They will occasionally build nests in bird-rooms. They need the same attention as olive and Cuban finches, although their cages should be somewhat bigger.

Green Jay, *Xanthoura luxuosa,* also called the Mexican Jay. 11 in. From Texas to Guatemala. Several varieties. **Pileated Jay,** *Cyanocorax chrysops.* 14½ in. Southern Brazil, Uruguay, Paraguay. **Greater Bird of Paradise,** *Paradisea apoda.* The male in breeding dress, including the tail, measures up to 40 in. Female reddish-brown above, lighter below, head and throat dark. New Guinea and neighbouring islands. The bird in the illustration comes from the Aru Islands. **Blue-green Magpie,** *Cissa chinensis,* also called the Hunting Cissa. 15½ in. Himalayas to China and Thailand. Several varieties. **Red-billed Blue Magpie,** *Urocissa occipitalis,* also called the Occipital Blue Pie. 24 in. Himalayas to northern Thailand and China. **Black-headed Magpie,** *Gymnorhina tibicen.* 16 in. Southern Australia. Two other breeds have white and grey backs. **Grackle** or **Tiong,** *Gracula religiosa.* 12 in. Southern India to southern China, Malay Peninsula, Borneo and Philippines. Many varieties. The bird in the illustration is the Greater Grackle from Malaya and Indonesia. The Indian species are smaller, and the smallest Grackles occur in southern India.

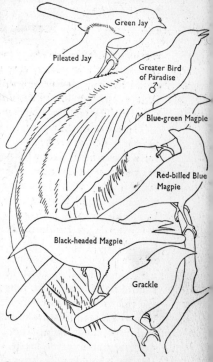

The buntings are noted for their brilliant plumage. They need a lot of light and a varied diet if they are to retain their bright colours. Therefore, improve the standard diet for exotic finches with plenty of green food, some fruit and berries, and also give them a good soft mixture, ants' eggs and mealworms. Males are kept in individual cages of 24 in. length, and pairs need more space. Buntings will do best in an aviary or in a bird-room. The males do not get on together; pairs build their nests in branches and, while rearing their young, are given soaked seeds, fresh ants' eggs, hard-boiled egg, egg-loaf and mealworms. They are now protected in North America and are therefore only imported very rarely. The gaily coloured non-pareil bunting also occurs in South America, where there is little protection for birds, and is offered for sale more frequently. The rainbow bunting appears in pet shops quite often.

The diuca finch, a peaceful, tame and friendly bird, is given the same diet as crested finches. Its cage must be 30 in. long for a single bird, somewhat longer for a pair. If diuca finches are to breed, they need a small aviary, covering an area of roughly 2 sq. yd., where they can build their nest in a roller travelling-cage. They will rear their young on mealworms, beetles, larvae and insects of every kind.

Cardinals are handsome birds and good, if not spectacular, singers. They can be kept in large cages, but will do better in a large outdoor aviary, where they may also breed. A cage for a single bird—if it must be kept in such confined space—should be at least 30 in. long; for the larger varieties, such as the red or Virginian cardinal, at least 36 in. Cardinals should be given a seed mixture of millet, crushed wheat, clipped oats and rape, and, in addition, a soft mixture of ants' eggs, gentles, grated carrot, cream cheese and egg-loaf. They should also have ripe fruit, berries of every kind, green food and leaf buds, which they love to crush in their bills. For rearing the young, they need extra mealworms, and other live insects, chopped hard-boiled egg mixed with cream cheese, and fresh ants' eggs. The red cardinal is the largest member of this group. He has also been called the Virginian nightingale for his song. Red cardinals should have sunflower seed included in their seed mixture. They are aggressive towards other aviary inmates during the breeding season. Each breeding pair should therefore be given an enclosure of its own, where the nest will be built amongst the branches or in a roller travelling-cage. The red cardinal can winter in the open in southern England; many birds have lived to an age of over twenty years in captivity. The slightly smaller green cardinal is much duller and is no great singer. It must be kept indoors and protected from frost during the cold season. The red-crested cardinal, too, is not noted for its song. Although hardier than the green cardinal, it should not be exposed to frost in our climate any more than the pope cardinal. The yellow-billed cardinal is more delicate and seems to be more of an insect-eater than the other varieties. Given the right setting, red, green and crested cardinals will readily breed in captivity; other birds of this group generally fail to do so. The incubating period lasts about a fortnight in the case of the crested cardinal. The young are ready to leave their nests two weeks later.

The saffron finch, from South America, is a popular cage-bird, for its plumage no less than for its voice. In winter, feed it on millet, maw and rape seed, a soft mixture, a lot of green food and unripe seeds. The saffron finch has frequently bred in cages and bird-rooms. It builds its nest in nesting-boxes or roller travelling-cages. While rearing their young, the parent birds should be given an additional soft mixture of chopped hard-boiled egg, egg-loaf and fresh ants' eggs.

Two Asian buntings, the red-headed and the black-headed, are regularly imported. They are fed like our native buntings, i.e. chiefly with seed in winter, and with a soft mixture in summer. They should also have plenty of green food and un-ripe seeds. The black-headed bunting is the better singer of the two.

The tanagers live on all kinds of fruit rather than on seeds and soft food. Give them chopped apples, pears, bananas, dates, figs, raisins and sultanas, cut oranges and tangerines, and a mixture of grated fruit, egg-loaf, ants' eggs and grated carrot. They are great eaters and digest their food with surprising speed, even for birds. The superb tanager is given less fruit, but more soft food. Other tanagers will chiefly get a good soft mixture, consisting of cream cheese, ants' eggs, egg-loaf, grated apple or carrot, and, in addition, chopped fruit and berries. The violet tanager is also fond of mealworms. One mealworm a day is considered sufficient. Cages for single birds should be between 24 and 32 in. long, according to the size of their in-mates. Tanagers are difficult to feed in a bird-room and should not be kept there. Pairs can be kept in outdoor aviaries during the summer.

The dwarf quail, usually called the Chinese painted quail,

from Asia and Australia, can be kept in a large lark cage, with a wax-cloth roof. For a pair, such a cage must be at least 40 in. long, 16 in. wide and 12 in. high. Dwarf quails can also be kept in an aviary, which must not be too crowded since, being ground birds, they would get badly soiled by the droppings of other birds. Diet and rearing are discussed in the chapter on pheasants (p. 152). A breeding pair should have a minimum area of 2 sq. yd.

The smaller exotic pigeons are quite suitable for cage and aviary, if no more than one pair is kept in the same enclosure. The comparatively large collared turtle-dove has become a much-loved domestic pet over the years. It will breed in a cage that is only 40 in. long. Although the smaller varieties —above all the Passerine ground dove, the Talpacoti ground dove, the diamond dove, and the tambourine dove—will also take to life in such a small cage, they are much happier in indoor aviaries and bird-rooms. If they are given small boxes as bases for their nests, they will soon breed. Further details will be found in the chapter on pheasants (p. 152).

PARROT-LIKE BIRDS

The fear of psittacosis has discouraged many bird-lovers from keeping parrot-like birds. A ban on the import of parrot-like birds was introduced. At present, birds can only be imported under licence. Most of the birds now available in the British Isles will have been raised in captivity or will be old residents, who should be fairly immune against psittacosis—a disease which can be just as easily, or more easily, transmitted by other birds. It was formerly called ornithosis, when it occurred in pigeons, turkeys, chickens, geese, egrets, etc., but it is now accepted as coming from the same virus. Psittacosis can easily be transmitted to human beings and domestic animals. Ex-sufferers can act as carriers long after they have recovered. In the past, many victims—almost a third—died. Since then, certain antibiotics have greatly reduced mortality. Between 1930 and 1953, 450 cases had occurred in the United States amongst human beings. Out of these, 14 were attributed to parrots and 172 to parakeets; 182 cases were attributed to infection from other birds, mostly pigeons and turkeys; some sufferers were infected at second hand, or from unknown sources. Yet although 40 per cent of all American poultry are thought to be carriers, mortality amongst human sufferers was no more than 6 per cent in 1947. This, of course, is still high enough, and makes psittacosis a justly dreaded disease. To prevent it, we must take reasonable precautions and know its symptoms. The parrot keeper, above all, should immediately get medical advice if he has any symptoms of influenza, and should mention to his doctor the possibility of psittacosis. Only birds in obvious good health should be acquired and great care should be taken over newly imported birds and birds from large bird farms. It is really best to obtain birds only from breeders or dealers of the highest repute. Any bird showing the slightest symptoms of illness must be carefully segregated—under no circumstances must it be kept in the living room—and a veterinary surgeon

Laughing Kookaburra

Blue-throated Barbet

Cock-of-the-Rock ♂

Green-breasted Pitta

Laughing Kookaburra, *Dacelo gigas*. Also called the Laughing Jackass. 18 in. Australia, Tasmania. Other Kookaburras—some of them in magnificent colours—are occasionally imported. They are smaller than the Laughing Kookaburra, but larger than our related native Kingfisher. **Blue-throated Barbet,** *Megalaima asiatica*, also called *Cyanops asiatica*. 9 in. From Kashmir to southern China and Thailand. Several varieties. Other barbets are occasionally imported from Africa, Asia and America. They require the same kind of attention as the Blue-throated Barbet. **Cock-of-the-Rock,** *Rupicola rupicola*. 11½ in. The female duller, dark olive-green shading to brown above, lighter below. **Green-breasted Pitta,** *Pitta cucullata*, also called *Pitta sordida c.* 6¾ in. Eastern Himalayas, Thailand, Malacca. Other Pittas, some of them brilliantly coloured, are imported from southern Asia.

---

must be called at once. We must also remember to wash our hands immediately after handling such a parrot. Cleanliness, ample space and good food, and the isolation of all newcomers until they are proved healthy are the best preventive measures.

Parrots can be kept on stands, or perches, as well as in cages or aviaries. Indeed, a larger bird will be happier on a stand, where it can stretch its wings, than in a small cage. A stand is only suitable for bigger birds, i.e. for those of at least African parrot size. A swing is suspended by two hooks on a gallows-like structure (see ill. p. 134). Food and drinking bowls are placed at opposite ends, and the bird itself sits on a thick wooden bar, which is firmly held in position by the ends of the U-shaped metal rod. Such swings can be bought at most ironmongers or pet stores. The chain should be galvanised and about 3 ft. long, i.e. long enough to allow some exercise, but

Toco Toucan, *Rhamphastos toko.*
23 in. Brazil to Bolivia, northern
Argentine. **Green-billed Toucan,**
Rhamphastos discolorus. 19½ in.
South-eastern Brazil, Paraguay.
The Aracaris, smaller relations of
the Toucans, need the same food
and attention. They also come
from South and Central America.
Senegal Coucal, *Centropus senegalensis.* 15 in. From West Africa
to Angola and Rhodesia. Several
varieties. The Coucals belong to
the same family as the Cuckoo.
Several other varieties are occasionally imported. They usually need
the same diet as the Senegal Coucal,
although the smaller breeds must
have a highly nutritious soft-food
mixture. **Knysna Touraco,**
Turacus corythaix. 18 in. South
Africa. Other Touracos, of equally
attractive colour, are frequently
imported and need the same attention as the Knysna Touraco, as
do their less spectacular relations,
the Plantain Eaters and the Go-away Birds.

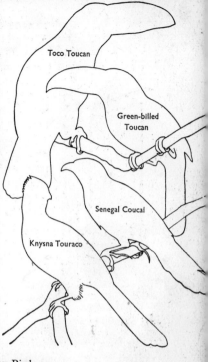

Toco Toucan

Green-billed
Toucan

Senegal Coucal

Knysna Touraco

---

not so long that the parrot can hurt itself when it tries to fly.
To prevent twisting, the ends are secured by swivelled catches
to a couple of steel split rings. One of these rings is fastened to
the leg of the bird—not, of course, to the leg used for holding
food—the other to the perch. Parrots quickly get used to being
chained and soon learn to climb back to their perch, if they
happen to dangle from it head-downwards after attempts at
flying. It does the parrot no good if its swing is moved to and
fro.

A stand consists of a vertical pole, attached to a base. It has
wooden bars screwed into it, along which the bird climbs with
the help of its beak (see ill. p. 134). We can also use natural
wood, with branches screwed into it at regular intervals (see
ill. p. 135). Food and water containers are secured firmly to the

top bar or branch. Parrots are not chained to stands and can be left to move about the room, as long as nothing valuable is within reach, because they are great lovers of fine leather bindings, which they will eagerly nibble to pieces with their strong beaks.

Whether parrots are to be kept in aviaries, large cages or small cages, depends on whether they are required as pets or as breeding stock. These two functions cannot be combined successfully. Many larger breeds, especially the African grey, mate for life. Tame birds are usually taken from their nests, are hand-reared, and therefore become attached to their keepers.

If they remain within the same family, they often become very devoted to a particular person, whom they almost consider the equivalent of a wife or husband.

A parrot stand

They show greater reserve towards other people, treating them rather like members of the flock, to which a pair would belong in freedom. But parrots can also get extremely jealous and may consider human beings as rivals in the affection of their owner. It was once thought that female parrots grew very attached to men, and males to women. This has been proved wrong. It is now clear that a bird's preference merely depends on whether it was reared by a man or a woman. When two tame birds get together, they generally show no interest in each other at all, and seem to prefer human company. But when they do mate—

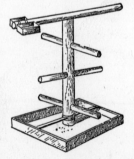

Perch with feeding bowls

although this is a very rare occurrence—they soon lose interest in their keeper and behave like a normal pair.

If we intend the bird to be a household pet, it must have a spacious galvanised wire cage—not less than 24 in. long, 14 in. wide and 16 in. high for a short-tailed parrot, like an African grey, an Amazon or a cockatoo—with a tall sheet-metal base, containing an easily sliding drawer. Some wire-netting is occasionally fitted above the drawer to prevent the bird from walking in its own droppings. Wooden cages are unsuitable, because they would soon get bitten to pieces. Since all parrots love climbing with their beaks and feet, they get quite a lot of exercise on the bars of their cage, and only need one thick perch, fitted lengthways, unless we prefer to give them two perches fitted in the ordinary way. It is best to use branches of non-poisonous deciduous trees—oak, ash, elm, lime, beech, etc.—for this purpose, so that the birds can safely nibble. Cages for long-tailed breeds, such as macaws, must be

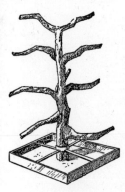

Another type of perch

at least 40 in. long, 24 in. wide and 24 in. high, and should only contain one perch.

Many cages have a perch above the roof: as soon as we open the door, the parrot climbs out, makes for the perch and frequently soils his cage. If we want to give the bird an outing, it is better to provide a free-standing perch or the type of stand shown on p. 134. It is often very difficult

Metal cage for parrots

to get a parrot back into its cage. Usually it can be manoeuvred back with a wooden bar, to which it is encouraged to climb. Having got there, it is transferred to the cage, where some special titbit awaits the 'prisoner', who would otherwise never

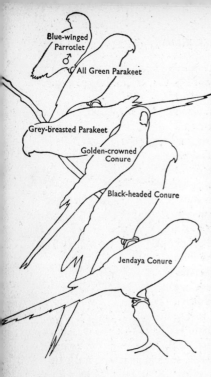

Blue-winged Parrotlet, *Forpus vividus*. 5 in. Southern Brazil, Paraguay. The similar Guiana Parrotlet, from north-eastern Brazil and Guiana, has a green rump, as has the female Blue-winged Parrotlet. **All Green Parakeet,** *Brotogeris tirica*. 11½ in. Eastern and southern Brazil. **Quaker** or **Grey-breasted Parakeet,** *Myiopsitta monachus*. 11½ in. Southern Brazil to eastern Bolivia and northern Argentine. **Golden-crowned Conure,** *Aratinga aurea*. 11½ in. Guiana to Paraguay and Bolivia. **Black-headed** or **Nanday Conure,** *Nandayus nenday*, also called *N. nanday*. 12½ in. Paraguay. **Jendaya Conure,** *Aratinga jendaya*. 12½ in. Eastern Brazil. Several other breeds of conure used to reach Europe regularly before the ban on the import of parrots, amongst them the Cactus, the Brown-eared and the Mexican Conure. They all need the same food and accommodation.

---

return to his uninteresting home. The cage door must always be securely fastened, since parrots are very clever at escaping. If a bird should fly out of the window, place the open cage, complete with full food and drinking vessels, on the window-sill or balcony. The parrot will usually return when it feels hungry, though often only after some days.

Parakeets, lovebirds and budgerigars will breed in cages without difficulty. A pair of budgerigars can breed in a cage no more than 30 in. long, 12 in. wide and 16 in. high, provided there are two nesting-boxes, one fitted to the outside of each narrow end of the cage. It is not advisable to keep more than one pair of parrots per cage or aviary if quarrels are to be avoided. Only budgerigars are more sociable. A cage 40 in. long, 20 in. wide and 28 in. high is sufficient for three pairs. An

Severe Macaw, *Ara severa.* 20 in. Panama to Bolivia, Amazon. **Hyacinthine Macaw,** *Ara hyacinthina,* also called *Anodorhyncus hyacinthinus.* 36 in. Central Brazil. **Military Macaw,** *Ara militaris.* 26 in. Mexico to Peru and Bolivia. **Red-and-blue Macaw,** *Ara chloroptera.* 32 in. Guiana to Bolivia and Uruguay. **Red-and-yellow Macaw,** *Ara maccao.* 34 in. Mexico to Bolivia. **Blue-and-yellow Macaw,** *Ara ararauna.* 36 in. Panama to Bolivia, Amazon. Some other varieties were occasionally imported in the past. Although many Macaws reach western Europe today, they cannot be imported into a number of countries without a special permit, which, in Britain, is quite easy to obtain. Macaws only rarely breed in captivity. Most of the birds offered for sale were taken from their nests and are therefore very tame. The larger birds, in particular, often become very attached to their keepers and love a lot of attention.

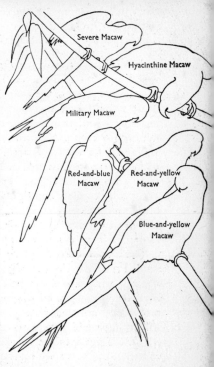

aviary will hold more, although six pairs should be considered the maximum in any enclosure. Here, too, supply each pair with two nesting-boxes, to avoid quarrelling. Great care must be taken to sort out birds that eat their own eggs. They are hard to trace and can thwart a breeder's efforts completely.

Cages where single pairs have nested successfully in the past have had the following dimensions

	Area	Height
Golden-crowned conure	60 in. × 20 in.	56 in.
Lovebirds	30 in. × 16 in.	20 in.
African grey parrot	60 in. × 30 in.	50 in.
Rosella	80 in. × 24 in.	40 in.
White cockatoo	100 in. × 60 in.	72 in.

These are approximate dimensions. Breeding in cages is only successful with tame birds. Generally, parrots are more likely to breed in aviaries which are at least 6 ft. high and cover a minimum area of 7 sq. yd. Details about constructing such aviaries are given in the chapter on pheasants (p. 152). But we must never forget that parrots have strong beaks and love gnawing wood. It is therefore better to use ½- to ¾-in. wire-netting (to keep out sparrows and rats), and metal tubing or angle iron for the framework. A third of the aviary is roofed, and the rear wall, as well as a third of the sides, are closed, thus giving some shelter against the weather. Planting an aviary with conifers and shrubs serves no purpose, because the birds would destroy everything. Small trees would only have a chance of survival in an under-occupied enclosure, inhabited by budgerigars, conures and lovebirds.

The tray of a breeding cage should be generously filled with sand. Fresh branches, arranged horizontally and changed frequently, will serve as perches. These branches, complete with bark, leaves and leaf buds, provide the birds with something to nibble and are thus both food and a source of amusement. Millet, rape and lettuce should be sown in flat seed boxes, which are put into the aviaries. The birds having eaten the contents, the boxes are removed again. It is quite possible to keep parrots and pheasants in the same aviary or bird-room, if we restrict ourselves to one breeding pair of each, except in the case of budgerigars.

The Quaker, or grey-breasted, parakeet is the only nest-building member of the parrot family; all other breeds nest in hollows. The minimum dimensions for nest-boxes are given below:

| | Nest-box | | |
	Area	Height	Inlet diameter
Budgerigars, Parrotlets, Lovebirds	5 × 5 in.	10 in.	1½ in.
Golden-crowned conure	7 × 7 in.	12 in.	3¼ in.
Severe macaw	13¼ × 13¼ in.	20 in.	6 in.
African grey parrot	10 × 10 in.	20 in.	4½ in.
Green parakeet	8 × 8 in.	12 in.	3¼ in.
Blossom-headed parakeet	7 × 7 in.	11¼ in.	2 in.
Rosella, Banded parakeet, Cockatiel	10 × 10 in.	14 in.	3¼ in.
Bourke's parakeet	7 × 7 in.	10 in.	2½ in.

Cockatoos and macaws will nest in eight-gallon barrels, whose inlet has been increased to a diameter of at least 6 in.

Lovebirds use all sorts of materials to line their nests. Some carry with their beaks, others with their claws. All other parrots—except for the already mentioned Quaker, or grey-breasted, parakeet—are without any constructive urge whatever. Their nest-boxes must therefore be filled with an inch-thick layer of sawdust to prevent the eggs rolling about. Quaker parakeets must have fir twigs—from which they will pick suitable pieces for their nests—in their aviary during the breeding season. They build spherical nests, preferably against the wire-netting in a corner.

Breeders must know the length of the incubating period and the age at which the young leave the nest.

	Incubating period	Age of leaving nest
Lovebirds	20–21 days	25 days
Grey-breasted parakeet	25–26 days	40 days
Golden-crowned conure	26 days	50 days
Black-headed conure	25 days	49 days
Severe macaw	24 days	49 days
Blue-and-yellow macaw	23–25 days	3 months
Blue-fronted amazon	30 days	62 days
African grey parrot	30 days	70 days
Fischer's lovebird	21 days	35 days
Blossom-headed parakeet	21–23 days	42 days
Rosella	20–21 days	31 days
Budgerigar	18 days	4–5 weeks
Banded parakeet	18–20 days	4½–5 weeks
Bourke's parakeet	17–18 days	4 weeks
Cockatiel	21 days	3–4 weeks

As a rule, the eggs are hatched only by the hen, who also takes care of the young single-handed for the first few days. The incubating period begins occasionally with the first egg, sometimes later. The time lag between the eggs of a clutch varies considerably: the smaller breeds usually lay an egg every day, the larger breeds every other day; for macaws and cockatoos the interval can be as much as a week. The young are therefore not hatched simultaneously and sometimes differ quite considerably in size and age.

Birds must not be disturbed during the incubating period. Looking into the nest may cause the female to abandon her eggs or even her young.

Hand-rearing is rather more difficult than in the case of other birds, because the parent bird takes the beak of the young into its own, and gurgitates the food into its crop. If, therefore, we have to act as a parent to a young parrot, we must take the food into our mouth, hold the beak of the fledgling in our lips, and force the pap down. But there are simpler and less repellent methods. We can hold the little parrot in our hand—having preferably waited until it is really hungry—and put its beak into a teaspoonful of the pap, which should be of body temperature. The spoon is then moved sideways, to and fro, until the bird has learnt to eat. Simpler still, we can feed it by using a syringe or with a thin, curved tube, filled with the food mixture. This tube is pushed down the throat as far as the crop, into which it is emptied. Care must be taken to stop the young from over-eating. Having fed them, place them in a dark box, lined with a soft material, which must be cleaned frequently. The birds like the dark. In their natural surroundings, they would grow up in dark hollows, without direct light. Hand-reared parrots still beg their keeper for food months after they have left their nest and only gradually get accustomed to feeding themselves.

If the young have been reared by their parents, remove them from the family enclosure as soon as they can feed themselves, so as to prevent them disturbing further broods.

Parrots live on ripe and unripe seed, green food, leaf buds, bark and fruit of every kind. The lorikeets also nibble the buds of flowers to extract nectar and pollen. Their food must be made up accordingly. Budgerigars are least trouble; they are content with a millet mixture (white millet, yellow millet, spray millet), kibbled oats and canary seed, and they will also rear their young on this diet. They further need green food (lettuce, chickweed, seeding grasses, etc.) especially when rearing their young, when they should also be given unripe seed (millet, grass, oats). Many breeders further add hard-boiled yolk of egg, ants' eggs, grated rusks, white bread soaked in milk, egg food and grated carrot.

Lovebirds, conures and the larger parakeets are given a seed mixture of millet, sunflower seed, oats and canary seed, with some hemp added, in winter, and large quantities of green food and fruit of every kind. During the breeding season and while rearing the young, the birds also need half-ripened seed, sprouting millet and, above all, green food. Many breeders also add egg, egg food and ants' eggs.

Amazons, macaws, cockatoos and African grey parrots get hemp, sunflower seed, oats, a little millet, wheat, peanuts and fruit, and, in summer, half-ripened maize (Indian corn), half-ripened oats and fresh twigs. Some egg food, stale white bread, and rusks can also be added.

In addition to their usual diet of millet, wheat, oats, sunflower seed, fresh fruit, bananas and berries, lories and lorikeets must have a porridge made by dissolving one soupspoonful of baby food or soaked breadcrumbs and two soupspoonfuls of condensed milk in a cup of hot water. This mixture should be well sweetened, and must always be absolutely fresh. For rearing, add ants' eggs, chopped egg yolk and egg food.

What kind of parrot-like birds should we choose? There are, first of all, the American breeds. Conures are hardy and breed without any difficulty in large cages. They are not really suitable for bird-rooms, where they will even attack stronger birds. Quaker parakeets can be kept in outdoor aviaries, summer and winter. Occasionally, they have even been allowed to roam. Birds let out of their aviary during the breeding season have invariably returned to their nests. Unfortunately, Quaker parakeets do a lot of damage to fruit and are therefore apt to be shot by the indignant owners of orchards. All green parakeets can be left to winter in the open. They, too, breed readily. Golden-crowned, jendaya and nanday conures are attractive and lively birds; golden-crowned conures will breed in large cages, the others will do better in aviaries. They all need frost-proof accommodation during the winter, which also applies to macaws. These, undoubtedly, are amongst the most handsome of all parrots. Some of them make delightful pets, while in others,

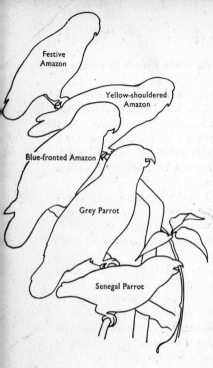

Festive Amazon

Yellow-shouldered Amazon

Blue-fronted Amazon

Grey Parrot

Senegal Parrot

Festive Amazon, *Amazona festiva.* 14 in. Amazon. **Yellow-shouldered Amazon,** *Amazona barbadensis.* 13¼ in. Venezuela. The Yellow-fronted Amazon, *Amazona ochrocephala,* is larger, with red shoulders and wing bars. **Blue-fronted Amazon,** *Amazona aestiva.* 15¼ in. Central Brazil to northern Argentine. The Cuban or White-fronted Amazon, *Amazona leucocephala,* from Cuba, is as big as the Yellow-shouldered Amazon. It is green, except for its white forehead and red throat and cheeks. **Grey Parrot,** *Psittacus erithacus.* 14 in. West and Central Africa. Several varieties, amongst them the smaller and darker *Psittacus erithacus timneh,* from Liberia and Sierra Leone. **Senegal Parrot,** *Poicephalus senegalus.* 9¼ in. West Africa. Several varieties, which mostly differ in the colour of the underparts. The bird in the illustration comes from West Africa.

---

alas, good looks are not matched by an equally attractive disposition. They grow into 'grumpy' creatures and screech all day and attack everybody within reach. We must, of course, appreciate that some noise is the price to be paid for owning such a fine creature. Occasionally, a macaw may prove to be an excellent talker. The severe macaw is the smallest bird in this group. Like the military macaw, it is not very brilliantly coloured. The red-and-yellow macaw, red-and-blue macaw and blue-and-yellow macaw are truly spectacular birds. The hyacinthine macaw, unfortunately, is hard to obtain and is very expensive. The amazons, of which there are many varieties, make good talkers and pleasant companions. Blue-fronted, festive, and yellow-shouldered amazons are frequently imported to Europe, although they can only be brought into the British Isles by special licence, in common with other

Ringneck Parakeet, *Psittacula krameri*. 16½ in. The female lacks the rose-pink neckband and the black streak below the face. Southern Asia, tropical Africa. The bird in the illustration is the *P. k. manillensis*, from southern India. **Plum-headed Parakeet,** *Psittacula cyanocephala*. 14½ in. The female has a bluish-grey head and lacks the rust-red shoulder patch. Southern India, Ceylon. **Eastern Rosella,** *Platycercus eximius*. 12½ in. The female somewhat duller. South-eastern and eastern Australia, Tasmania. Several varieties. **Peach-faced Lovebird,** *Agapornis roseicollis*. 6¾ in. South-west Africa. **Fischer's Lovebird,** *Agapornis fischeri*. 6 in. Lake Victoria (East Africa). **Masked Lovebird,** *Agapornis personata*. 6 in. Southern Tanganyika, Nyasaland. The Masked Lovebird is closely related to two other Lovebirds, also with white rings round their eyes: the Nyasa Lovebird, *Agapornis lilianae*, with pink cheeks and forehead (south-east Africa) and the Black-cheeked Lovebird, *Agapornis nigrigenis*, with brown head and reddish-brown throat. **Red-faced Lovebird,** *Agapornis pullarius*. 5½ in. The female duller. West Africa (Loango to Ghana). The Madagascar Lovebird, *Agapornis cana*, from Madagascar, has a grey face.

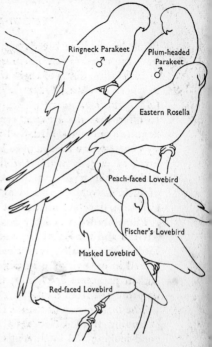

Ringneck Parakeet ♂

Plum-headed Parakeet ♂

Eastern Rosella

Peach-faced Lovebird

Fischer's Lovebird

Masked Lovebird

Red-faced Lovebird

---

parrots and parrot-like birds. They will settle down happily to life in spacious cages, but must be kept in heated rooms during the winter. Provided this condition is observed, they may well survive several owners.

African grey parrots are extremely long lived and make excellent talkers, but are sensitive to cold. They have many smaller relatives, amongst them the Senegal parrot. Senegal parrots, who learn to talk occasionally, are kept in cages of a minimum length of 20 in., a width of 12 in. and a height of 16 in. Lovebirds, in popularity next to budgerigars, also come from Africa. Five breeds and twelve different varieties have been imported so far. These small parrots can be kept in cages or in aviaries. Some of them will breed readily, amongst them Fischer's lovebird (*Agapornis fischeri*), and the masked lovebird (*Agapornis personata*), which, unfortunately, has been crossed so often that the greatest care must be taken if we wish to acquire a pure-bred bird. Red-faced and peach-faced lovebirds, by contrast, are always pure bred; but while the peach-faced lovebird breeds without difficulty, the red-faced lovebird will do so only very rarely in captivity. It is largely a question of luck. Lovebirds should also winter in frost-proof rooms, although, once acclimatised, they are quite hardy.

Plum-headed and large Indian parakeets, no less than the African and the Asian ringneck, are amongst the finest aviary birds. Occasionally, they also learn to talk. Only specimens reared in captivity are suitable for cages. Ringneck and large Indian parakeets are hardy; the plum-headed parakeet must be protected from frost.

The large group of the cockatoos, which come from an area extending from Celebes to Australia, also includes many good-looking and intelligent creatures. The larger breeds are chiefly suitable for stands, perches and cages. If they are to breed, they need fairly spacious aviaries. The smallest kind, the pretty roseate cockatoo, will be content with a cage of the type used for a Senegal parrot. Rose or salmon-crested and greater sulphur-crested cockatoos need more space. The cockatiel is now considered a member of the cockatoo family, although it was formerly classed amongst the Australian parakeets. It is a very popular cage-bird, thanks to its hardiness, its modest requirements and, last but not least, its pleasant disposition. It also breeds readily and is therefore ideally suited for pheasant enclosures. Hand-reared, it will grow into a tame and affectionate bird. A cage measuring 32 × 16 in. with a height of 20 in. is considered adequate.

Many Australian parakeets are beautifully coloured. They are kept in cages and aviaries all over the world. Unfortunately, some of the most beautiful breeds have been almost exterminated in their native country, where they are now protected.

In consequence, they are almost impossible to obtain. The most famous representative of this group is the budgerigar, which has become one of the most popular domestic pets within less than a century. John Gould, the great naturalist, brought the first specimen to England in 1840. Thirty years later, thousands of pairs were imported every month, until the Australian government imposed an export ban in 1894. To-day, budgerigars are bred almost exclusively in captivity; indeed, new strains are even sent to Australia, where there is a ready market for them amongst bird fanciers.

Budgerigars bred in captivity in England soon after the arrival of the first specimen; by 1855 they were breeding in Germany. A yellow strain was produced in 1872, a blue strain six years later, and white birds were first bred successfully in 1920. Innumerable new varieties have made their appearance since, amongst them the cinnamonwing, the grey, the opaline, the mauve, the whitewing, the albino, the olive-yellow, the cobalt, etc., to name only a few. Beginners should, at first, breed without paying attention to colour. When they have become real enthusiasts, they will soon be captivated by the laws of heredity and will try to discover more about them. There is no shortage of good textbooks on this subject.

Young, hand-reared budgerigars are extremely tame and friendly and can be left to fly around the room. Some of them make amusing talkers. Thanks to their tremendous fertility, budgerigars are to-day the cheapest parakeets on the market and can frequently be bought for a few shillings. Yet the first pair to be sold in England changed hands for £26! Budgerigars are bred in cages and aviaries, which can be shared by several pairs, if there is sufficient space. Breeding pairs of other Australian parakeets can share an enclosure with pheasants or doves, etc., but not with their own kind, or with related birds.

Redrump parakeets are hardy and present no special problems to the amateur. The other Australian parakeets should have frost-proof shelter in winter. Although they do not normally suffer greatly in our climate, they might come to harm during really sharp frosts. The most handsome varieties are the king parakeet, crimson-winged parakeet, banded parakeet, rosella parakeet, pennant's parakeet and Stanley parakeet. The lively little grass parakeets are extremely pretty, but rather expensive; the more soberly coloured Bourke's parakeet is less striking in appearance, but cheaper.

When rearing their young, all these parakeets need far more green food, sprouting, germinated and unripe seed, millet, grass seed, oats, sunflower seed, shepherd's purse, chickweed, etc., in addition to their normal diet, than do other parrots. Some breeders also add mealworms, ants' eggs, egg, egg food and rusks; others reject such an 'unnatural' diet and consider extra seed and green food sufficient.

Lories and lorikeets come from Australia and the islands of the Indian Ocean; some varieties have bred in captivity. Their feeding habits—they need a kind of porridge, which they lap up—make them rather more of a problem in captivity than other parrot-like birds. They also excrete much more frequently. Yet their striking colours have gained them many friends in the past, when there were no import restrictions. Lories can be kept in individual cages; tame birds will breed in a cage measuring $40 \times 40 \times 40$ in. They can also be kept in bird-rooms, where, of course, they must not be joined by any other parrots. In winter, lories and lorikeets need a heated room; in summer, they can live in outdoor aviaries. Another attractive member of this group is the mountain lory, of which there are several varieties throughout Australia and the islands of the South Pacific.

Many people would like to own, or even train, a talking parrot. This should not be too difficult. Birds with a fairly large vocabulary are frequently offered for sale and a dealer of integrity should be able to procure such a parrot sooner or later. But do not be upset if the new acquisition takes some time to display its accomplishments in new surroundings. A far greater disappointment may follow, when it becomes obvious that both accent and choice of expression are the products of an obviously unfortunate early environment. If we want a parrot to 'pass muster' in respectable, if not necessarily good, society we must either rear a baby bird by hand—this would more or less limit us to budgerigars, since nestlings of other breeds are extremely hard to obtain—or get a bird that is still too young to have mastered bad language. Such a parrot should then be kept completely cut off from other birds—whose voices he must not hear—and given as much attention as possible. Every parrot is able to imitate other birds, but not necessarily human speech. We must again and again repeat the word, or the sentence, we want him to say, or the tune we would like him to whistle. There is no sense at all in punishing the pupil, if he cannot learn, because this would merely frighten him. All efforts may seem in vain for months, until, suddenly, the parrot talks. His vocabulary will be limited, although some birds will master over a hundred expressions. Patience and endurance are everything. It is entirely a matter of ability whether a parrot will ever talk or not and we should therefore not make him suffer if he lacks 'talent'.

Some pheasants are brilliantly coloured, others are less spectacular, although beautifully marked. Most birds of this group are hardy, long-lived and breed easily, if we know how to look after them. The amateur should start with hardy breeds from cold climates before venturing with the more delicate tropical birds. Hardy pheasants are ideal for any outdoor aviary or enclosure. Certainly they will need quite a lot of space. Their aviary should cover a minimum area of 14 × 20 ft. and should be about 7 ft. high, but not higher, because the impact of the

Sparsely planted pheasant aviary, a third of which has a solid roof

birds, rising in flight when something has frightened them, would be too much and they might get badly hurt.

The aviary must, above all, afford complete protection from rats, foxes, cats, ferrets, etc. It is best to begin by excavating all round to a depth of about 30 in. for the foundations, as shown in the drawing on p. 153. Concrete should then be poured in and when it has hardened an 8 in. wall of brick or concrete is raised to a height of 16 in. The enclosed area is filled with an 8 in. layer of gravel or builder's ballast. Two-thirds of the aviary, i.e. an area roughly 14 ft. square, is then fenced in and roofed with wire-netting. The framework either consists of angle iron or metal tubing. An iron band is fitted

to the framework at a distance of half an inch above the base
and the wire-netting attached to it. If this band were omitted,
or placed directly on the concrete, the danger of corrosion
would be increased considerably.

The wire-netting itself should be galvanised and of a fairly
thick gauge, and between ½-in. to ¾-in. mesh. A less closely

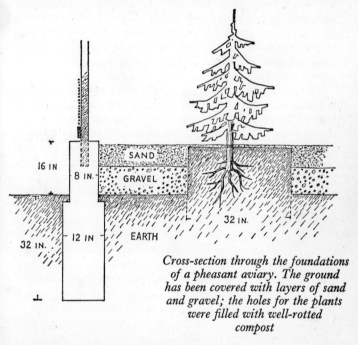

*Cross-section through the foundations
of a pheasant aviary. The ground
has been covered with layers of sand
and gravel; the holes for the plants
were filled with well-rotted
compost*

meshed wire might give easy access to mice, rats and sparrows.
The latter are not only interested in the pheasants' food, but
are also carriers of all sorts of diseases, from fowl pest to the
dreaded gape-worm (*Syngamus tracheus*), and must therefore
be kept out completely. The remaining third of the aviary is
built in brick and given a solid roof.

The best type of aviary roof is tiled. The battens for the
tiles will have been laid on an intermediate wooden roof,

constructed by nailing boards across the beams. Although this may sound rather elaborate, it is not an unjustifiable extravagance. If a tile should crack, or be blown away, the boards will stop the birds escaping. We can, of course, use roofing-felt instead, but a felt roof is never a sound proposition. Unless a wooden inner roof is properly tongued and grooved, the wind, blowing through the cracks, may tear the felt, which, in any case, will have to be tarred every two years. A tiled, or slated, roof is beyond doubt the best solution, not least because it is easy to repair. It is, unfortunately, rather expensive. Corrugated asbestos and corrugated iron have many virtues from a purely practical point of view, but are ugly.

The brick part of the aviary, which will also contain a door, is rendered, pointed or white-washed. The roof must extend beyond the aviary, if the water is to run off properly. The covered section is concreted over an area of roughly a square yard, where food and water containers are placed. The roof shelters the food from the rain and also protects the birds from the elements. Perches—up to $2\frac{1}{4}$ in. in diameter, according to the size of the birds—are placed as close under the roof as possible. The birds will sleep there undisturbed during the night, even if a cat or a stoat should try to climb up on the wire. The birds' droppings will fall on dry ground, where they can be easily cleared away and the aviary inmates will even be able to take the sand-baths they love so much under cover. If we only keep pheasants, no perches will be needed, except under the roof.

A detachable piece of wire-netting is fitted to allow us to get into the cage without causing too much disturbance when we want to replace the soil with all its accumulated dirt, maggots and breeding places for disease. This should be done every spring and, preferably, also in autumn.

Many bird-fanciers use wood for the framework; but, however carefully treated, it rots sooner or later, causing annoyance and expense. Furthermore, many pheasant aviaries are shared by parrots and budgerigars, who will welcome the timber frame as a pleasant addition to their diet. The Author has seen wooden structures, costing hundreds of pounds, disintegrate beyond repair within a few years.

Timber aviaries are by no means more 'natural' than metal-framed enclosures, as has been suggested. They may perhaps look better at first, but they soon become a prey to the weather and acquire a hovel-like, neglected appearance. The more solidly we construct the aviaries, the cheaper they will be to maintain.

Planting, too, is not merely a question of satisfying our sense of beauty. Many a bird-lover imagines that a miniature park complete with trees, shrubs, perennials and lawns will be appreciated by his birds as much as by him. But we must remember than an area of under 30 sq. yd. will be occupied by two, three, or four pheasants, who are used to very much more space in their natural setting. The lovingly planted trees will be completely soiled, the lawn scratched and pecked. Within a short time, everything will look scruffy and ugly, and, worse still, the health of the birds will suffer, since a closely planted aviary is very hard to clean. It is therefore better to put down a thick layer of sand, leaving only two or three holes, to be filled with humus and planted with conifers, preferably Serbian spruce or Austrian pine. The sand is afterwards raked close to the trees. But these trees have no function, except to please us. The birds can easily manage without them. In a thickly planted aviary, the birds like to hide and remain, or grow, very shy; but they quickly get accustomed to human beings in an open setting.

Fresh green food should be given with their ordinary food. It will be much healthier for the birds than the stale and dirty grass in which they run about. If we like, we can fit an open concrete trough for drinking water near an outer fence in the uncovered section of the enclosure. A piece of metal tubing, for draining, will lead from the bottom through the concrete base to the outside, where it will be closed with a stopper, allowing us to empty the trough for cleaning, etc. We must, of course, keep it empty if there is any danger of frost, when the drinking water for the birds should be put into saucers or small bowls.

The aspect of an aviary is most important. There should be protection against wind, which means that the enclosed portion will usually face north or north-west. Rain, in the British Isles, usually comes from the west, and would therefore leave the roofed-in area unaffected. One or two trees, planted on the south side, will give shade. We must, however, avoid fast-growing varieties, like poplars, which can be a danger to the foundations of any fairly new building. Robinias, or locust trees—also called false acacias—are to be preferred, because they grow rather slowly and throw a light, instead of a dark, shade. The soil, in consequence, dries out much quicker after rain.

If several aviaries are being built, do not place them too close to each other. Most pheasant cocks of the same, or a related, breed get on well enough, as long as no hen is present. Female company makes them fight each other desperately, even if they are separated by wire-netting. They will run along the fence opposite the 'enemy's' enclosure, quite beyond themselves with rage, and oblivious to hunger and thirst. Two adjoining aviaries should therefore be divided by a 2-ft. high screen of timber, sheet metal, or some kind of wall to keep the hostile cocks out of each other's sight. But such screens are not always beautiful and many people therefore keep their aviaries some distance apart, planting the gaps with fast-growing hedges.

If space is scarce and the aviaries must be close to each other, the best solution is to link them with a covered, enclosed walk, where food, and equipment, etc., can be kept. This will also prevent the birds from escaping when we have to open the aviary doors—normally an extremely tricky process, calling for the utmost care.

Beginners often imagine an outsize aviary, where as many birds as possible can flutter around just as they would in nature, as the ideal setting. But in nature there is much more space, even when birds congregate in large flocks. The emptier the aviary, therefore, the healthier it will be for each inhabitant. It is easier to keep clean and the danger of infection is much smaller. Each bird can easily get at food and water, can be better observed and is more easily caught in an emergency. More pleasure is obtained if the birds can be observed properly.

An open, partly roofed aviary is sufficient for all hardy

pheasants. The tropical and sub-tropical breeds, such as Mikado, Elliot's and Swinhoe pheasants need a frost-proof shed, which, in the case of Argus and peacock pheasants, must also be heated in winter. Although they do not need excessive warmth, the temperature should not be allowed to fall below 10 deg. C. (50 deg. F.). Such a shed, leading off the aviary, is not difficult to construct. An area of 10 sq. yd. is sufficient for smaller breeds, but peacocks need more space; their shed should measure approximately 5 × 4 yd. The brighter their shed, the better the birds will get through the winter. A skylight would be ideal, but ordinary windows are quite sufficient. The cheapest source of heat is an iron stove, or a Courtier stove, both of which need little attention. All stoves and pipes must, of course, have a wire guard around them to protect the birds from getting hurt. Central heating is even better—it can be linked to the heating system of the house—if we can possibly afford it.

The shed is also given a thick layer of sand, perches must be fitted, and food and drinking vessels must be arranged to prevent their getting soiled by the birds' droppings. Any further equipment only takes up valuable space and would be in the way when cleaning out. To guard against frost, the walls should be fairly low, not more than 6 ft. 8 in., and should be well insulated, possibly of cavity brick construction, lined with asbestos and rendered. Wood is not to be recommended. Although it offers good insulation, if both sides of the framework are faced with tongued and grooved matchboarding and the space between is lined with peat, it is also most attractive to rats and mice. This, indeed, applies to all timber construction. Glass wool, in place of peat, is better, but still does not afford absolute protection.

It is useful to have a small anteroom partitioned off from the peacocks' quarters with wire-netting. The stove can be safely kept there, as can food, a small incubator, etc.

Pheasants are fed on grain, soft food and as much green food as possible. Their grain mixture consists of barley, wheat, hemp and millet, and, in winter, Indian corn. Omit hemp and Indian corn during the laying season, and add more millet and green food. Tropical pheasants also get carrots, cut-up apples and boiled parsnips. There are many commercial soft foods on the market. These mixtures should be slightly moistened and given warm in winter, cold in summer. They must not be wet and sticky, but should have a fairly loose consistency, and can be enriched with salt, dried ants' eggs, and maize. In summer, the pheasants should also get cut-up grass, lettuce, chickweed and dandelion; in winter, germinate some wheat in a warm place and either feed it to the birds when it has just begun to sprout or when it has grown to a length of 4 in. If the wheat is required merely to sprout, put it into flat wooden boxes and keep it damp; if it is to shoot, sow it properly in seed boxes—which are kept in the open—and water it regularly. The grain mixture is put into troughs, so that the pheasants can feed without being able to walk about and scratch amongst their food. Soft food—no more than the birds will eat within the next quarter of an hour—is given once or twice daily. It must not be left standing in the open for too long in winter; frozen food is extremely bad for all birds. There must always be enough drinking water, because a pheasant needs a lot of liquid to soak the hard grains in its crop. Special care must be taken to supply water frequently in winter to make sure that the birds do not go thirsty when everything is frozen.

The aviaries are cleaned out thoroughly every spring, as soon as the danger of frost has passed. The sand is changed completely, the perches are cleaned, or replaced where necessary, the entire structure is minutely examined for damage, repaired and, if possible, re-painted. A pair, or a cock and two or three hens, are then placed in each aviary. For good results, cocks should not be used for breeding before their third summer. Hens already lay in their second year, but will also do better if kept a little longer.

When buying new birds, examine them very carefully for defects. Claws and legs should be well formed; overgrown beaks are a sign of old age, as are excessively horny legs. Pheasants travel in a hay-lined basket with a piece of sacking sewn on to it as a cover. Birds can only share a basket if they are used to each other, although there is a certain risk attached to it even then. Adult birds are really always best sent on their own. An open box, covered with sacking, and close-meshed wire-netting above the sacking as protection, can be used instead of a basket. The birds should be left to eat and drink well before their journey and should, if possible, be despatched in the evening, to arrive in the morning.

New arrivals must be introduced very carefully to their aviary. This should always be done in the morning, to give them time to feel their way around. At first, open the travelling-box or basket only sufficiently for the bird to get out. Then place the container, complete with inmate, in the aviary, withdraw and wait, until the new bird leaves its box, or basket, of its own free will. If the bird is made to get out, it may flutter about madly with fear and might easily come to

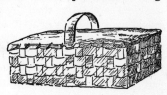

Travelling-baskets for pheasants

harm; also, leave the bird alone for some time after arrival. If it remains very timid, screen the aviary all round with conifer branches or straw matting. The matting is removed in stages, and the branches will become bare in the course of time. The curtain is thus gradually lifted, while the pheasant is becoming accustomed to its new quarters.

The utmost care must be taken in matching pairs or in changing breeding arrangements. Some cocks are extremely hostile towards all hens, chase them at every opportunity, and may even kill them. Impeyan pheasants have an especially bad reputation in this respect. It is not unusual for cocks to kill any hen within reach. Quite often, a pair may have lived together peacefully for years, when, suddenly, 'war breaks out' between the sexes. Much care is therefore required if tragedies are to be avoided. Such 'bluebeards' are fortunately rare amongst other breeds. Generally, each aviary will be stocked with one cock and two or three hens. Eared pheasants, tragopans, and peacock pheasants are kept in pairs, an arrangement that will also prove more acceptable to Kaleege and silver pheasants.

Having thoroughly cleaned the cages in spring, prepare the nesting and laying places for the hens. Fir branches should be placed in a corner against the wire-netting to provide a shelter, just big enough for a single bird, with only a narrow inlet. Here, the hens will scratch a hollow in the ground for their eggs. Remove these daily and mark them in pencil (*not* with ink, indelible pencil or a ball-pen) with the date and the breed of the hen. They are then removed to a cool place, stored in chaff and replaced in the nest by plaster eggs. This prevents the birds from eating their eggs—an easily acquired habit that would make all one's efforts futile.

Rearing is easiest if it can be left to the hen. Small aviaries, unfortunately, are not suited to large families. The eggs are therefore hatched in an incubator or given to a broody hen. The eggs of larger breeds, such as Impeyan and eared pheasant, can be entrusted to the hens of the larger domestic varieties, such as Sumatra and Yokohama, or even turkeys. Other eggs are given to bantams or bantam crosses. The approximate number of eggs of each breed and the length of its incubating period are listed below:

	Number of eggs	Incubating period
Ring-necked pheasant	8–15	24 days
Reeves' pheasant	7–15	25 days
Elliot's pheasant	6– 8	25 days
Northern peacock pheasant	1– 2	21 days
Golden pheasant	9–15	22 days
Lady Amherst's pheasant	6–12	23 days
Mikado pheasant	5–10	27 days
Kaleege pheasant	6–12	25 days
Swinhoe pheasant	6–12	25 days
Eared pheasant	5– 8	27 days
Impeyan pheasant	6– 8	26 days
Peacock	6– 8	28 days
Red jungle fowl	6–10	19–20 days
Domestic fowl		21 days
Turkey		28 days

The foster-mother is removed from the nest for half an hour every day, when she is allowed to roam and scratch around the chicken yard, where she can eat and drink her fill. If she is given eggs of several varieties to incubate, make sure that all the chicks will hatch at the same time. The hen would otherwise leave the nest with the early arrivals and abandon the eggs. She is therefore first given eggs that take longer to incubate, and others are added later. After eight or ten days, examine the eggs for the first time by looking at them through a cardboard tube against the electric light (see ill. p. 63). It is soon possible to tell if there is any life. The bad eggs with watery yolks are at once discarded. This examination is repeated after another week. It is desirable to set several hens simultaneously, so that clutches, reduced by the removal of dead or sterile eggs, can be combined, thereby freeing some of the hens. These can immediately be given more eggs to hatch. No hen must have more eggs than she can cover comfortably. If some of the eggs feel rather cool, the clutch is too large. The hens are given a quiet, sheltered place in their shed for incubating. The nests should be as wide apart as possible to prevent the birds from disturbing each other.

If pheasant hens are allowed to hatch their own eggs, all other pheasants should be removed from the aviary. Hens often try to sit on each other's nests, which only leads to quarrels. Some cocks are good fathers, amongst them the white-crested Kaleege pheasant, who even looks after his young, but most of them have little family feeling, and may even peck at their children, and should therefore be segregated.

If the eggs are to be hatched by domestic fowls or turkeys, young and foster-mother will have to get used to each other. For the first few days, keep the young in a small box, covering an area of about 24 × 24 in. It must be large enough to hold bowls for food and water, in addition to the mother hen. The floor should be coated with a thin layer of sand. It is necessary to find out if any of the young chicks are trying to shelter under the hen. If they do so, hold them against the protecting feathers, until they recognise the source of warmth and comfort. Hen and chicks will be accustomed to each other after three or four days, when they can be transferred to a larger enclosure.

Two things are of the utmost importance in rearing pheasants: dry, warm weather, and a diet including as many ants' eggs as possible. The young birds stand the damp very badly

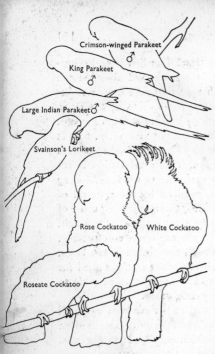

Crimson-winged Parakeet, *Aprosmictus erythropterus*. 13¼ in. The female duller. Eastern Australia, northern Australia, New Guinea. **King Parakeet,** *Alisterus scapularis*. 14¾ in. Female with green head, neck and breast. Eastern and south-eastern Australia. **Large Indian Parakeet,** *Psittacula eupatria*. 19 in. The female lacks the black stripe on the cheeks and the red neckband. Ceylon, India to Indo-China. Several varieties. **Swainson's Lorikeet,** *Trichoglossus haematodus*, also called Blue Mountain Lory. 13¼ in. Southern Australia, Victoria, New South Wales. Many varieties. The bird in the illustration comes from eastern Australia. **Roseate Cockatoo,** *Cacatoe roseicapilla*. 11½ in. Australia. **Rose** or **Salmon-crested Cockatoo,** *Cacatoe moluccensis*. 20 in. Ceram and Amboina. It closely resembles the White-crested Cockatoo, *Cacatoe alba*, 18 in., from the Halmaheira Islands. **White Cockatoo,** also called Great Sulphur-crested Cockatoo, *Cacatoe galerita*. 19 in. Australia, Tasmania, New Guinea. Except for size, it resembles the much smaller Lesser Sulphur-crested Cockatoo, *Cacatoe sulphurea*, 13½ in. from Celebes, Buton and the Togean Islands.

and are—in contrast to chickens and turkeys—mainly insectivorous in their early life. Unfortunately, the weather cannot be changed. The chicks are therefore kept for a fortnight in a dry, light and airy shed; they are only then allowed outdoors, where they will at first occupy poultry runs. These are 2 ft. high wire enclosures covering an area of 2½ × 1½ yd. Chicken runs have no floors, but are moved to fresh patches of ground from time to time. The roof is formed by two hinged flaps, which act as doors. A rearing coop will adjoin one of the narrow ends of the run. This coop, 1½ yd. long and 1 yd. wide, has a wooden

Canary, a domestic pet bred from the Serin. The **Belgian Canary** is a sport deliberately produced by breeders. The **Harz Roller** is chiefly noted for its song; the **Orange Canary** is the product of a cross between a canary hen and a Red Hooded Siskin. It is one of many variants, bred especially for their colour. **Budgerigar,** *Melopsittacus undulatus.* 8½ in. In the female, the skin near the beak is yellowish-grey. Australia. The Budgerigar, in its wild state, is chiefly green. Over the years breeders have produced yellow, blue and many other shades. Breeders' associations have set up standards for size, shape and colour, both for canaries and budgerigars.

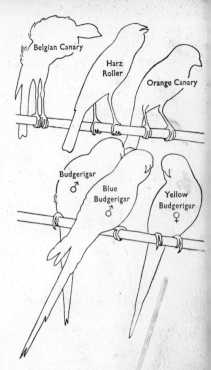

floor, small glass windows and a roof in the form of a trapdoor. It is divided by wooden bars, spaced sufficiently wide apart to allow the chicks, but not the hen, to move from one section to the other. A hinged flap divides coop and run, which are moved to fresh ground every two or three days. This provides the young pheasants with shelter and an opportunity to find insects in the grass. In warm weather, the chicks will run around their enclosure with or without their foster-mother. Food and water are placed in the run in separate bowls for old and young. The bowls for the chicks must be kept under protective wire-netting to prevent the hen from getting at them. The nights, or cold spells, will be spent in the coop by the whole family. The chicks will run to and fro, seeking shelter under the hen, or eating their special food in their own section. When it rains, cover the entire run with a tarpaulin; the birds will also need some protection in excessively hot spells. When they no longer need her warmth, the young pheasants are separated from the hen and are put into aviaries, where they will grow up without any extra attention.

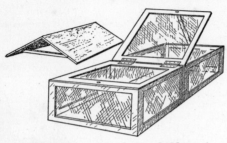

Pheasant coop with detachable roof

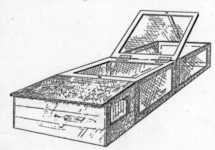

Run with rearing coop

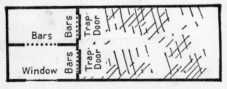

Plan of coop and run. The coop is further divided by bars

During the first few days, the chicks are given fresh ants' eggs every two hours. The hen is allowed to share these meals, because the young birds' attention will be drawn to the food if they see their foster-mother eat. If ants' eggs are not available, use a mixture of finely chopped hard-boiled egg and finely crumbled white bread, always adding some green food such as dandelion, chickweed and yarrow. After ten days, the young are also given a good soft food, which must be moist and crumbly. They are now only fed four times a day, and should have some buckwheat gruel and peeled millet added to their soft food, which must always be absolutely fresh, just as the containers must be absolutely clean. Ants' eggs can be supplemented with a little minced lean raw meat, if necessary.

The problem of finding ants' eggs is solved by placing inverted flower pots near ants' nests. After some time, the ants will deposit their eggs in these hide-outs, and we can transfer them directly to a bucket. They are then immediately given to the chicks. The more of these ants' traps we provide, the easier it will be to rear pheasants.

Young pheasants grow rather slowly. They can already flutter about after ten days, but it takes at least three months before they are really independent.

Occasionally, chicks are hatched artificially in heated incubators, where they are also reared, unless it is preferred to let a hen rear them with her own brood. But this has its problems, because the hen can soon distinguish between her own chicks and the little pheasants, whom she will probably attack. It is therefore advisable to let the foster-mother hatch the young pheasants, if we want her to have motherly feelings towards them.

If it is decided to use a brooder-heater—a type of lamp used for rearing, of which there is a great variety on the market—place it in a small box, with a layer of sand at the bottom. The chicks are placed in this box and are put again and again near the lamp, until they accept it as the source of all warmth and will approach it on their own initiative. It will be necessary to supplement this mother substitute by pretending *ourselves* to peck at the food with a small stick, just as a real mother or foster-mother would peck at it with her beak. Eventually, this method will teach the young pheasants to feed themselves. Heater and birds are moved to a bigger nest-box after two or three days, and, again, to a run after a fortnight. But this method is rather laborious and is only suitable for large concerns, where pheasants are reared commercially and have the attention of a full-time staff.

Where it is at all possible, the eight- to ten-week old pheasants should be left to run around a fairly large enclosure, planted with a few shrubs and trees, but not too much

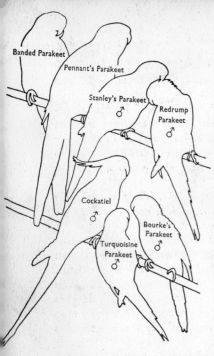

Banded Parakeet

Pennant's Parakeet

Stanley's Parakeet ♂

Redrump Parakeet ♂

Cockatiel ♂

Bourke's Parakeet ♂

Turquoisine Parakeet ♂

Banded Parakeet, *Platycercus xonarius*, also called *Barnardus zonarius*. 15 in. South, central and north-western Australia. The Ringneck Parrot, *Platycercus barnardi*, also called *Barnardius b.*, with green head and a red stripe across the forehead, comes from south-eastern Australia, and the Twenty-eight Parrot, with black head and a red band above the beak, from south-western Australia. **Pennant's Parakeet,** also called Crimson Rosella, *Platycercus elegans*. 13½ in. East and south-eastern Australia. Many varieties, amongst them the Adelaide Rosella, *Platycercus elegans adelaidae*, from southern Australia. It is orange, instead of red, with a lighter shade of blue. **Stanley's Parakeet,** *Platycercus icterotis*. 11 in. The female somewhat duller. South-western Australia. **Redrump Parakeet,** *Psephotus hae-matonotus*. 11 in. The female has a green rump, otherwise greyish-olive instead of bright green. Southern Australia. **Cockatiel,** *Calopsitta hollandicus*, also called *Leptolophus hollandicus*. 12½ in. The female less brilliant. Australia. **Bourke's Parakeet,** *Neopsephotus bourkii*. 9 in. Western and central Australia. The female duller and without a blue band above the beak. **Turquoisine Parakeet,** *Neophema pulchella*. 9 in. The female less conspicuous, without the reddish-brown wing patch, throat and the breast greenish, rather than yellow. Southern Australia. Similar varieties include the Splendid Grass Parakeet, *Neophema splendida*, from southern Australia, with bright blue face and scarlet throat, the Elegant Grass Parakeet, *Neophema elegans*, also from southern Australia with blue streaks above the beak and the eyes, yellowish cheeks, green breast and a yellow patch on the belly, and the Blue-winged Grass Parakeet, *Neonanodes chrysostomus*, from southern Australia and Tasmania. This bird resembles the Elegant Grass Parakeet, except for its yellow eye streak and sulphur yellow belly.

Kestrel, *Falco tinnunculus.* 13½ in. Head and tail of the female brown instead of bluish-grey. British Isles, Europe, Africa, Asia. Many varieties. The bird in the illustration comes from Central Europe. **Hobby,** *Falco subbuteo.* Male 13 in., female 14½ in. British Isles, Europe, northern Asia, north-west Africa. Several varieties. The bird shown occurs throughout Europe and the British Isles. **Barn Owl,** *Tyto alba.* 13½ in. World-wide distribution. Many varieties. **Tawny Owl,** *Strix aluco.* 15¼ in. British Isles, Europe, Asia, to China and India, north-west Africa. **Little Owl,** *Athene noctua.* 8¾ in. British Isles, temperate zone of Asia, North Africa. **Long-eared Owl,** *Asio otus.* 14½ in. British Isles, Europe, temperate zone of Asia, North America, North Africa. Several varieties. Many birds of prey and young owls are hard to identify when they are still covered in down. They all need the same food and attention, if they are to do well.

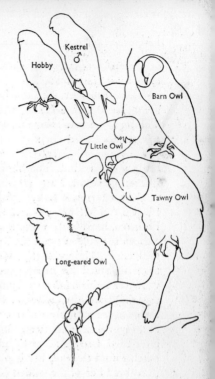

undergrowth, which would merely encourage their natural elusiveness. They are at first let loose with their foster-mother, who is later removed. Unless there is no opportunity for the birds to escape, one wing will have to be clipped. This must be checked from time to time, since pheasants moult after the first three months, when the clipped feathers will be replaced.

The common pheasant gives least trouble. The breed found most frequently on private shoots is a mixture of three separate varieties, namely the bronze-necked pheasant, from the Caucasus, the Mongolian pheasant, from the region south of Lake Balkash, and the ring-necked pheasant, from China. However pretty these hybrids may be, they are of no interest to the serious breeder, who is concerned only with pure-bred varieties, or their different sports, such as a white or green bird, also known as 'tenebrosus'. Buy, therefore, only from the most reputable breeders. All these pheasants are very hardy and will breed readily, if sufficient trouble is taken in the beginning. The Japanese versicolour pheasant is more delicate and needs a frost-proof shed during the winter.

The long-tailed breeds are amongst the most handsome birds of their kind. The hardiest of them is the magnificent Reeves' pheasant. Fully grown cocks need large cages, because of their enormous tails, which can exceed a length of 5 ft. Elliot's and Mikado pheasants, both from southern China and Formosa, need fairly warm sheds in winter.

Both the golden pheasant and Lady Amherst's pheasant are very hardy. Unfortunately, they cross easily and crosses continue to breed for many generations. They are of no value whatever to bird-fanciers. Impure Lady Amherst's pheasants, especially, are often offered for sale; usually, the underparts of the cock are not pure white, or the green crown contains some red. Hybrid hens are more difficult to identify. The hen of the pure-bred Lady Amherst's pheasant has a bluish-grey bare patch round the eye, her legs are blue horn-colour, while the pure-bred hen of the golden pheasant has no bare patch round the eye and has yellow horn-coloured legs. Lady Amherst's pheasants are often quite aggressive; new aviary inmates must therefore be kept under close observation for some time.

White-crested, lineated and Nepal Kaleege pheasants, and the silver pheasant, are all closely related. They are long lived and present few problems. White-crested and Nepal Kaleege pheasants and silver pheasants stand up to our climate extremely well; the lineated Kaleege pheasant should have a frost-proof shed in winter. The Swinhoe pheasant is even more delicate. Here, too, it is necessary to take great care over purchases. Pure-bred specimens of the Nepal Kaleege pheasant and the closely-related fire-back pheasants are hardly ever obtainable in Europe. Beginners should therefore not buy them at all. White-crested Kaleege pheasants are occasionally not quite pure; lineated and silver pheasants are usually fairly safe.

Eared pheasants, tragopan and Impeyan pheasants, all birds

of the mountains and highland plateaus of Asia, will stand any temperature. Pallas' eared pheasant breeds readily; the Manchurian eared pheasant is, unfortunately, less obliging. Both varieties like to dig about with their beaks. They should be given lots of green food, particularly grass turves, of which they are very fond.

The Impeyan pheasant is a bird of outstanding beauty. It digs intensively and will take bulbs and roots out of the ground with its beak. It, too, needs green food and lawn turves. Cocks and hens frequently do not get on together, and care must be used when pairing birds. Aviaries for Impeyan pheasants should be as large as possible—the bigger the better. The brightly coloured tragopans also need a large enclosure, and much green food, leaves, buds, fruit and berries. Eared pheasants and tragopans are kept in pairs, as are Impeyan pheasants, provided they get on together. In a large aviary—50 sq. yd. and over—two hens for each cock can be provided.

The small peacock pheasants or Polyplectrons from the tropical zone of south-east Asia are most delightful creatures. Rather sensitive to cold, they need a heated shed in winter. Only bantams can be used as foster-mothers, ordinary domestic hens being too large. The chicks are at first unable to pick up food from the ground, and expect to take it from their mother's beak. Since our domestic poultry do not feed their own young in this manner, it is necessary to give the little peacock pheasants ants' eggs, cut-up mealworms, etc., with a pair of tweezers until, after about a week, they are able to feed themselves. They may even have to be fed forcibly at first. They should not have to share their foster-mother with other chicks. Most probably they would get the worst of things if they were reared with more aggressive birds. Peacock pheasants generally make good mothers. Each enclosure will only hold one pair, since even the hens of this breed do not live well together. The cocks spread their tails like peacocks at display.

Peacocks can be left to roam, especially the Indian variety (*Pavo cristatus*, the common peafowl). They do not breed too readily in aviaries, where they are given the same type of food as pheasants, except that they should have coarser grain, no

hemp or millet and as much green food as possible. The young
are reared exactly like pheasant chicks.

The common peafowl has been kept for its beauty since
time immemorial; wild birds are long-legged and more slender
than their domesticated cousins. A peacock, complete with tail
and head, formed the *pièce de résistance* of the Elizabethan
banquet. Fortunately, it is almost inedible and therefore es-
capes the fate of other, scarcely less handsome, creatures. The
larger and even more splendid green peafowl—whose female,
in contrast to other varieties, resembles the male, except for the
absence of the train—needs a heated shed in winter.

An aviary for peafowl must be fairly spacious—at least 50 sq.
yd.—to give these large birds sufficient opportunity for exercise. The chicks are kept inside for a few days and are then put
into runs. Weather permitting, they should be let out with their
mother as soon as possible. They will do much better if they can
forage in the grounds in search of insects and fresh green food.

Several other types of fowl need the same care and attention
as pheasants. The attractive red jungle fowl is an ancestor of our
domestic fowl. A suitable breeding stock will consist of one
cock and two or three hens per aviary. The domestic variety of
the Guinea fowl is well known. Its undomesticated African
cousin needs a frost-proof shed in winter if it is to survive for
any length of time. The hens are bad mothers, but rearing can
safely be entrusted to domestic hens or turkeys. The incubating
period lasts 24 days.

The francolin, a type of partridge, occurs throughout Africa
and southern Asia in many varieties. The black partridge, or
black francolin, from India is sensitive to cold, like all his
kind, but is otherwise not a difficult bird to keep. The young
should be hatched and reared by domestic fowls or turkeys.

Our native partridge is well suited to aviary life. A clutch
consists of between 10 and 20 eggs, and the incubating period
lasts 23 days. Two relations of the partridge, the red-legged and
the rock partridge, will also breed in aviaries, if we only keep
one pair in each enclosure. Partridges need a regular supply of
fresh grass turves. The rock partridge is extremely hardy; the
red-legged partridge must be protected from hard frosts.

Not everybody can afford to put up large pheasant aviaries. Different types of quail are therefore ideal for the bird-fancier of more limited means. Some varieties need very little space. The Chinese painted quail will be content with little more than 2 sq. yd.; our own native quail needs about 3 sq. yd.; California quail and Virginia partridge will thrive and breed in an area of 7 sq. yd. According to size, quails are given soft food and, in addition, small seeds like canary, millet, hemp and wheat. Their cage should provide some protection against sun and wind, and should also give them some cover, since they love hiding in tall grass in their natural surroundings. The ground is coated with a thick layer of sand. It is most useful to attach a small shed, or pen, to the enclosure, into which the birds can be driven to avoid upsetting them when the aviary is cleaned. Quails are highly nervous creatures and should not be excited unnecessarily. California quail and Virginia partridge need perches; the other breeds can manage without them.

If the quails are required to breed, partly cover the ground of the aviary with turves and plant a few small shrubs amongst them. The hens will scratch out a nest, if there is cover. They breed readily and are good mothers. It is best to let them rear their own young, since even bantam hens are too large and heavy for the delicate little quail chicks, who might easily come to harm. It must be remembered that the cocks of the Chinese painted and California quails and of the Virginia partridge help to rear the young, while the cock of our natve iquail is a danger to his offspring and must be removed as soon as the hen starts laying. Size of clutch and length of incubating period are listed below:

	Size of clutch	Incubating period
Chinese painted quail	8–12 eggs	17 days
Quail	10–15 eggs	20 days
California quail	10–20 eggs	23 days
Virginia partridge	10–20 eggs	23 days

The young Chinese painted quails are fully fledged after two months; other breeds take one or two weeks longer. The rearing diet should include, above all, fresh ants' eggs, a little chopped hard-boiled yolk of egg, green food and, later, very small seed.

Pheasants, partridges and quails will chiefly occupy the floor of the aviary. The space is therefore not fully used, and we can easily fill it with smaller birds, which spend little time on the ground. Many bird-fanciers like to have a pair of pheasants occupying ground level, a pair of pigeons or medium-sized parrots for the middle region, and, finally, one or two pairs of very small birds. More birds would only be a source of dirt and ill-health, because their droppings would soil the ground birds.

Make absolutely sure, therefore, that the pheasants' disposition is as attractive as their plumage, or they might be found pecking the weaker birds to death. There must, of course, be enough perches, feeding places and nesting places in the aviary.

Two or three large boughs, with their leaves already dried off, should be hung up against the wire-netting or on the ceiling in such a way that as many twigs as possible are in a horizontal position. Size and thickness will depend on the kind of birds to be kept. One of these boughs should be placed close to the roof to afford protection against rain. The food for the smaller birds is usually more expensive than that of the pheasants', who must therefore be prevented from eating anything not meant for them; they are also apt to peck at other birds during meals. The smaller inhabitants therefore have their food put into containers, attached to special frames, fastened high up on the wire-netting or to the roof, where the pheasants cannot get at them. These may be constructed of wire-mesh, battens or twigs, spaced close enough to admit only small birds. If, therefore, pigeons or budgerigars are kept in addition to pheasants, fit such a device for each of these groups so as to make quite sure that the smaller birds will not starve.

Pigeons nesting in the open need small low-rimmed wooden boxes, which are fitted close to the wall in the roofed-in section, and breeds nesting in hollows are given nesting-boxes. For stock doves, these should measure 10×10 in. (inside), at a height of 14 in. and with an inlet of $3\frac{1}{2}$ in. diameter. Aviaries for pigeons normally nesting in shrubs should contain some bushes or small firs, where wire baskets can be fitted as frames for the nests. All nesting-boxes and similar devices are removed and thoroughly washed with an insecticide at the end of the breeding season. Fir branches and boughs, serving as perches, must be replaced every six months.

Now for the pigeons themselves! Our native breeds present no difficulties whatever. They are hardy, breed readily and are easy to feed. The pink-headed dove is equally hardy. Though of Indian origin, it is an old-established domestic pet. It also occurs in a white variety. The stock dove, as already mentioned, needs a spacious nesting-box. Wood pigeon, collared turtle-dove, turtle-dove and pink-headed dove use boxes and wire frames as bases for their nests. Except for the wood pigeon, they use very little nesting material. The clutch of any pigeon consists generally of two and, less frequently, of one or three eggs. The incubating period lasts 17 days in the case of the domestic pigeon, 14 to 15 in the case of the collared turtle-dove, turtle-dove and pink-headed dove. The eggs of the wood pigeon take 15 to 16 days, and the stock dove's 16 days, to hatch. Incubation begins with the first egg; the second is laid after an interval of two days. In consequence, the young will not hatch simultaneously and will be of different ages. The chicks are inclined to leave their nests very early—long before they are fully fledged—and will sit on the ground, where they might easily get killed by the pheasants, unless they are put back into their nests.

All the pigeons mentioned above will eat the same food as the pheasants. If they are kept on their own, they should get the same seed mixture, supplemented with wheat, kibbled oats and rape seed. Pigeons also need green food, such as lettuce, chickweed and dandelion. There is no need for special rearing food, since the birds feed their young with the so-called 'pigeons' milk', an excretion from their crops. After a few days, they give them seed, which they also first soak in their crops. The turtle-dove has one or two broods during the summer, and other breeds have three or four, at times even five.

A number of very attractive doves come from the tropics.

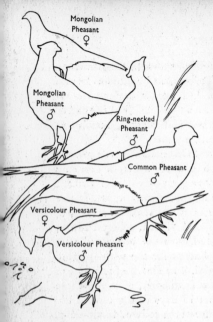

Mongolian Pheasant ♀

Mongolian Pheasant ♂

Ring-necked Pheasant ♂

Common Pheasant ♂

Versicolour Pheasant ♀

Versicolour Pheasant ♂

Mongolian Pheasant, *Phasianus colchicus mongolicus.* Male, 38 in. Originally Kazakhstan, Mongolia, northern China, now throughout British Isles, Europe and America. **Ring-necked Pheasant,** *Phasianus colchicus torquatus.* 30 in. (male); the female resembles the hen of the Bronze-necked Pheasant, but is lighter. Eastern China. **Common Pheasant,** *Phasianus colchicus colchicus.* Male 34 in., female 24 in. The female is light grey, mottled black and with darker wavy bands above, collar shot with red, yellowish-grey below. Western Asia, south-western shores of the Caspian. **Versicolour Pheasant,** *Phasianus colchicus versicolor.* 30 in. Southern Japan. *Phasianus colchicus* occurs in innumerable varieties throughout Asia, from the Caucasus to Korea, Japan and southern China. The pheasants found in Europe and the British Isles are a mixture of the four breeds mentioned above. Pure-bred pheasants are, unfortunately, extremely rare.

They are usually not hardy and suffer with the beginning of the cold season, when they should be placed in heated bird-rooms, or large cages kept in warm rooms. If they have been bred in an outdoor aviary, they should not have nesting facilities in their winter quarters. Further broods would merely exhaust them. The cages for smaller breeds, like the diamond dove, should be at least 40 in. long, 20 in. wide and 30 in. high. Larger birds need more space. Indeed, always provide as large a cage as possible for any kind of pigeon.

Diamond doves and Talpacoti ground doves breed readily in captivity. The tambourine dove is attractively coloured, the barred ground dove strikingly marked. The female of the Namequa dove is much less conspicuous than the male; the passerine ground dove and Inca dove are not much to look at, but their males have a rather pleasant breeding call. A far

Reeves' Pheasant, *Syrmaticus reevisi*. The male up to 84 in., female 30 in. The inconspicuously coloured hen can be recognised from the markings on the head; the upper portion is reddish-brown, sides and neckband black-brown, eye streak, throat and a ring round the throat yellowish-brown; otherwise grey-brown above, and mottled yellowish-brown below. Interior of northern China and central China. **Elliot's Pheasant,** *Syrmaticus ellioti*. Male 32 in., female 20 in. The basic colour of the female is brown, with lighter and darker hues. Some black, streaked with white, above, tail chestnut, with whiter tips and black bands. Eastern China, south of the Yangtse River. **Mikado Pheasant,** *Syrmaticus mikado*. Male 34 in., female 22 in. Head and upper neck of the female are reddish-brown, breast brownish-grey, belly brown, wing coverts black, mottled reddish-yellow. Back and rump mottled black and rust, tail brown, banded reddish-yellow and black. Formosa.

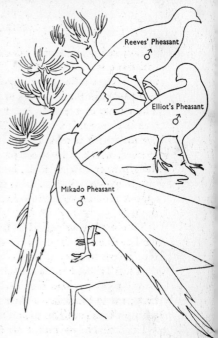

larger bird, the little brown dove, also breeds without difficulty and is comparatively hardy. All these breeds are far surpassed in looks by the bleeding heart doves, who owe their name to the extraordinary red patch on the breast. It is quite possible to look at a bird repeatedly without realising that it is not badly hurt. Bleeding heart doves will give little trouble if they are kept in a heated room in winter and are given the right food.

All tropical pigeons need millet, wheat, rape seed, poppy seed and buckwheat, the larger breeds getting more wheat, kibbled peas and kibbled oats. In addition, they must have green food occasionally, also ants' eggs and a little soft food. They also like a little rock salt. For rearing, add chopped hard-boiled egg, ants' eggs, an insectivorous mixture and cut-up mealworms. The young birds must have animal proteins if they are to thrive.

Tropical pigeons may raise as many as three or four broods in the summer. They all breed in the open and therefore should have roofless roller travelling-cages, open boxes and wire baskets placed in the branches or against the sides of their aviary. The chicks of bleeding heart doves should be reared by domestic pigeons. It might thus be possible to obtain two clutches per month; it is most important to make sure that the foster-mother, who has been set on the eggs, will give her charges their proper rearing food, instead of forcing hardly anything but grain—which does them no good—down their crops. The eggs of medium-sized breeds can be entrusted to pink-headed doves.

The incubating period lasts 13 days in the case of diamond, tambourine and little brown doves, a fortnight in the case of the Talpacoti ground dove, and 16 days for bleeding heart doves. All these breeds are fully fledged—bleeding heart doves after 6 weeks, others even earlier—after a comparatively short time; many birds leave their nest after a fortnight, although their parents continue to feed them.

Unfortunately—except for tambourine and Namequa doves—males and females of most breeds are very much alike, and it is therefore very hard to tell whether we have a pair or merely two birds of the same sex behaving like a pair. Often, there are four eggs—two laid by each hen—or none at all. It is therefore advisable to place three or, better still, five birds in each aviary. As soon as one, or two, genuine pairs have come together, the surplus bird and one pair are removed, since no aviary should contain more than one pair of doves. Only the pink-headed dove is excepted from this rule. Several birds of this breed can be kept in one large aviary, although this is not likely to produce ideal breeding conditions.

The problem of sexing doves must be kept in mind when buying birds. It is not fair to ask a dealer to guarantee that he is really supplying a pair. Beginners should therefore buy direct from established breeders, if they want a well-tried breeding pair.

Parrots, as fellow-lodgers of pheasants, are discussed in the chapter entirely devoted to them.

If the aviary is to include smaller birds, in addition to pheasants and doves, choose some of the hardy native species—particularly seed-eating birds—which will also breed in captivity. Simply plant a few firs to give them sufficient cover for their nests. The rearing food for the young is placed in a device (see p. 176) which allows access to the parents, but not to larger birds. Our native thrushes also settle happily amongst pheasants. Jays look most effective in such a setting, as does a red-billed blue magpie, although the latter is a danger to smaller pigeons and young pheasants, and therefore cannot be kept with them. Tropical finches, also, should not be mixed with ground birds, who would wreak havoc amongst their young. But despite the risk inevitably attached to mixed aviaries, try to discover what breeds and individuals are suited to each other. The following ensembles of doves, song-birds, pheasants and budgerigars have proved entirely satisfactory in the past. Here are seven different possibilities for beginners, who can at the same time become acquainted with the abbreviations customary amongst dealers in birds. 1.0 golden pheasant means one cock; 0.1 golden pheasant one hen; 1.1 a pair. Therefore, 1.2 silver pheasant means one cock and two hens, and 3.3 budgerigar means three pairs.

1.2 Golden pheasant.	1.1 Turtle-dove.	1.1 Goldfinch.
1.2 Silver pheasant.	1.1 Little brown dove.	1.1 Siskin.
1.2 Lady Amherst's pheasant.	1.1 Stock dove.	1.1 Crossbill or Bullfinch.
1.1 Peacock pheasant.	1.1 Diamond dove.	1.1 Pekin robin.
1.2 Common pheasant.	1.1 Wood pigeon.	1.1 Brambling.
1.2 Mongolian pheasant.	1.1 Collared turtle-dove.	1.1 Redpoll.
1.1 Eared pheasant.	1.1 Namequa dove.	3.3 Budgerigar.

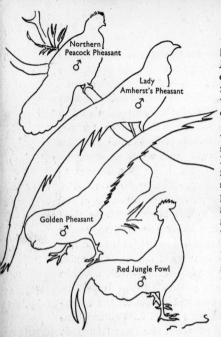

Northern Peacock Pheasant ♂

Lady Amherst's Pheasant ♂

Golden Pheasant ♂

Red Jungle Fowl ♂

Northern Peacock Pheasant, *Polyplectron bicalcaratum*, also called *P. malacensis*. Male 28 in., female 22 in. The female darker, with smaller and less clearly marked eyes and shorter tail. Southern India, Malay Peninsula. Several varieties. **Lady Amherst's Pheasant,** *Chrysolophus amherstiae*. Male 60 in., female 27 in. The female resembles f. Golden Pheasant, but is larger, with bare bluish patch round the eyes and blue-grey feet. Wings and tail banded grey, brown and black. Szechwan to northern Burma. **Golden Pheasant,** *Chrysolophus pictus*. Male 42 in., female 26 in. Female an inconspicuous greyish-brown with darker streaks and patches, tail brown and unevenly banded. Beak and feet a yellowish horn colour. Central China, further east than Lady Amherst's Pheasant. **Red Jungle Fowl,** *Gallus gallus*. Male 28 in., female 18 in., not unlike a similarly coloured bantam hen, but with a small comb and very small wattles below the chin. Neck and upper mantle black, edged with yellow, otherwise brown, with black and yellow patches above, reddish-brown below, vent almost black. Northern India to Java and Indo-China. The male of the Grey Jungle Fowl, *Gallus sonnerati*, is grey above and below, with black mantle, edged grey and mottled black and yellow, and has red and yellow patches on the wings. Lacks white patch of skin behind the ears. The male of the Javan Jungle Fowl, *Gallus varius*, from Java, has a bluish-red straight comb and no ear patch and is almost completely black, except for some yellow streaks and green reflections above.

Swinhoe Pheasant, *Lophura swinhoei*. Male 32 in., female 20 in. The female without a crest, dark brown with light patches above, lighter, with darker bands, below. Neck dark with light patches, wings very conspicuously banded black and yellowish-white. Red feet and eye-patch. Formosa. **Chinese Silver Pheasant,** *Lophura nycthemera*. Male 48 in., female 28 in. The female has a smaller crest. Olive brown above and below, with somewhat lighter throat. Breast and belly rather indistinctly streaked, beak horn-coloured, feet red. Southern India and southern China. Many varieties. The bird in the illustration belongs to the breed most frequently kept in Europe and comes from the region round Kwantung. **White-crested Kaleege Pheasant,** *Lophura hamiltoni*. Male 28 in., female 22 in. The female is reddish-brown, with grey-brown crest; back tipped darker, wing coverts lighter. Himalayas to Gharwal and Kashmir. **Burmese Silver Pheasant,** *Lophura lineata*. Male 28 in., female 22 in. The female has a dark crest and is brown, tipped with grey above and reddish-brown streaked white below. Throat whitish, feet grey-brown. Southern Burma. **Nepal Kaleege Pheasant,** *Lophura leucomelana*. Male 28 in., female 22 in. The female resembles the hen of the White-crested Kaleege Pheasant, but is darker, with more reddish-brown below. The four last-mentioned breeds are generally considered variants of one race.

CROWS AS PETS

A miserable black creature sits under a tree, its beak wide open: a carrion crow has fallen out of its nest and is now at the mercy of any cat, dog, or well-meaning child. This is an opportunity to acquire a friendly cheerful pet. Birds of the crow family are amongst the most intelligent and affectionate creatures. Hand-reared crows grow very attached to their keepers and remain tame and friendly all their lives. If they are not often found in people's houses, it is because they are fairly large, make a certain amount of dirt and are therefore not very suitable for the small house or flat of to-day. They hardly ever breed in captivity and therefore do not appeal to the fancier, who also wants to be a breeder. Yet crows deserve more popularity as cage-birds. They are not very hard to obtain, since carrion and hooded crows, jackdaws, magpies and rooks enjoy only very limited protection under the Protection of Birds Act 1954 and can be taken from their nests—in a humane manner, of course —by owners or occupiers of land. Other birds of this group are fully protected and may only be kept in captivity if they have been bred there.

Most hand-reared birds of the crow family will learn a few words. Although not exactly accomplished conversationalists, talking birds have great attraction for many fanciers.

Feeding is no great problem. They will eat mice, dead sparrows, meat, small fishes, vegetables, grain, some green food, berries, fruit—in fact everything edible. They can also be given left-overs from our own table, as long as they are not too heavily spiced or too salty. The remains of soft food and soaked dog biscuits are equally welcome. Occasionally, we can also make up a mixture of boiled potatoes, cut-up bread, soaked wheat grains, bran, some dog biscuits and a little meat. Where possible, also add tiny feathers, especially to the food intended for ravens and crows. Remember that all birds of this group love to hide left-overs, which may easily rot in crevices or gaps, if they are not carefully looked for when the cages and aviaries are cleaned.

The larger breeds, such as raven, carrion crow, hooded crow and rook, are best accommodated in out-door aviaries. For ravens, these should measure 14 × 5 ft., with a height of 6 ft. 8 in.; for crows 6 ft. 8 in. × 5 ft., with a height of 6 ft. Individual jays, magpies and jackdaws can also be kept indoors in a cage no less than 5 ft. long, 32 in. wide and 40 in. high. All these birds can be kept in the same enclosure, if they are roughly the same size, since smaller birds would get bullied.

Branches with a minimum thickness of $1\frac{1}{2}$ in. will serve as perches; a large bowl, filled with four inches of water, will be needed for bathing. If several jackdaws are kept in an aviary, including a pair of mature birds, fit a nest-box measuring 10 × 10 × 14 in. with an inlet $3\frac{1}{2}$ in. in diameter. There will be a good chance that the birds will breed, if they are given plenty of green food, mice and dead sparrows.

The largest member of this group is the raven, a handsome, intelligent creature, and also a talented vocalist. If a pair is kept watch their remarkable display, accompanied by the most extraordinary noises. Such a couple must have an entire aviary to themselves. Other birds would be persecuted and finally killed by the raven. An individual raven often becomes so attached to its keeper that it can even be kept at liberty. Watch them carefully, however, during the migrating season in spring and autumn, when they are apt to go very far afield. But, fond as one may be of the raven, one must appreciate that it is a great danger to young poultry and must always be kept under lock and key—albeit in very comfortable surroundings—near poultry yards.

Carrion and hooded crows are very easy to feed. Rooks breed in colonies, prefer a vegetarian diet and are very partial to sprouting grain. Jackdaws frequently nest on tall chimneys and towers, in contrast to magpies, whose nests are built in hedge-rows and even near houses. The jay, by contrast, is a forest bird, and builds a well-secluded and sheltered home for its young. It is very fond of ripe acorns.

If helpless birds are found and have to be reared, arrange

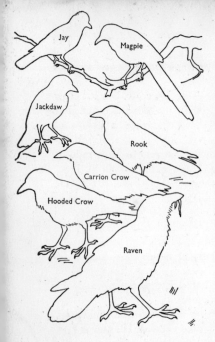

Jay, *Garrulus glandarius.* 13½ in. British Isles, Europe, temperate zone of Asia. Many varieties. **Magpie,** *Pica pica.* 18½ in. British Isles, Europe, Asia to Indo-China, west coast of North America. **Jackdaw,** *Coloeus monedula.* 13½ in. British Isles, Europe, Asia as far as Turkestan and Pakistan, north-west Africa. **Rook,** *Corvus frugilegus.* 18½ in. British Isles, Europe, temperate zone of Asia. **Carrion Crow,** *Corvus corone.* 19 in. British Isles, western Europe, as far as the Elbe and the southern and eastern ranges of the Alps. **Hooded Crow,** *Corvus cornix.* 19 in. Eastern Europe, from the Ural mountains to the Elbe, Italy. **Raven,** *Corvus corax.* 26 in. British Isles, Europe, North America. Two other black members of the crow family are the Cornish Chough, *Pyrrhocorax pyrrhocorax*, also called *Coracia p.*, 16 in., and the Alpine Chough, *Pyrrhocorax graculus*, also called *Coracia g.*, 15¾ in. The former has a slender, red beak, and occurs from the British Isles to China, the latter with its short yellow beak, from Spain to western China and also in the southern Alps.

---

some form of nest in a box. The birds will probably not open their beaks at first and must therefore be forcibly fed until they realise that their human foster-parent is the source of all nourishment. The more often they are fed at the beginning, the more they will thrive. They are, at first, fed every two hours with chopped mice or pieces of meat, bread soaked in milk, a little potato and bran, and some green food.

The tropical members of this group include the red-billed blue magpie, the blue-green magpie, the green jay and the pileated jay. The black-headed magpie from Australia is black and white and has a most attractive voice. All these birds can be kept in out-door aviaries in the summer, although they are not hardy—with the exception of the red-billed blue magpie—

and must be kept in frost-proof rooms during the winter. They can also be kept in single cages measuring at least $60 \times 32 \times 40$ in. Properly looked after, they will live many years. Red-billed blue magpies will breed in an aviary of not less than 5 sq. yd. if they have a dense shrub to build their nest in.

All these tropical birds need green food and a mixture of one part thrush food and two parts mashed potato, cut-up white bread, some raw meat, and coarsely ground maize, all moistened and enriched with oats, wheat and sunflower seed. The thrush food, which, as already mentioned, makes up a third of this mixture, is itself a mixture of two parts grated and squeezed-out carrot, one part ants' eggs, one part cream cheese and one part hemp flour. A branded soft food can also be used and improved with grated carrot or apple. Young mice, too, are always eagerly accepted.

Crows, without exception, need a lot of attention if they are to become or remain friendly and tame companions that give pleasure for many years.

Kestrels, tawny owls and long-eared owls are sometimes removed from their nests by ignorant people who may even imagine that they are doing good. We can prove our love of animals by rescuing and hand-rearing these unfortunate creatures. They should be placed in flat, hay-filled boxes and kept in a well-lit room. Such a box must not be put near anything greatly treasured, because even young birds of prey are apt to spatter their excrement over everything. If the birds are still very young, cover their box with a light-weight woollen shawl at night and provide some protection against cold. This will be no longer necessary when the feathers appear under the down. The little birds of prey are at first fed four or five times daily, later twice, and, finally, only once. If they are reluctant to eat, feed them forcibly by pushing some moistened food down their carefully opened beaks with tweezers or with the fingers, until they have to swallow. All kinds of raw meat will be welcome, including bits of intestine, glands, etc. Such scraps should first be coated with a little calcium food. Young mice or dead sparrows are even better. Old mice, too, are very nourishing. At first they are cut up, later they should be given whole. Owls swallow them as they are, falcons tear them up first. There are many ways of obtaining young sparrows, though some, undoubtedly, will not appeal to bird-lovers, who will prefer humanely trapped mice. If young sparrows are considered essential, they must be killed as quickly as possible.

Properly fed, the young owls and falcons grow their feathers rapidly and become very tame. They should still take their food from the hand—although by then only once daily—when they are fully fledged, if they are to remain pets. Even fully grown birds of prey must have freshly killed mice or sparrows once or twice per week in addition to butcher's meat, because they badly need the vegetable matter contained in the stomachs, intestines and bones. When they are a little older, young kestrels and hobbies frequently push each other out of their nests at feeding time. As soon as they are fledged, they are placed in an out-door aviary which should be $3\frac{1}{2}$ to $4\frac{1}{2}$ yd. long, 80 in. wide and 80 in. high. Several thick branches, arranged to allow as much uninterrupted flying space as possible, and a bathing trough are all they need. As always, part of the aviary must be properly roofed, and the rear end and one narrow end must be solid to give protection against the wind.

Our native owls frequently fall into human hands. They leave their nests long before they are fully fledged and then hover for hours, or even days, in the undergrowth. Young owls can easily be recognised by the colour of their eyes. The eyes of long-eared owls are orange, those of the little owl yellow, and those of the tawny owl and barn owl a browny-black. Barn owls nest in farm buildings, church towers, etc., little owls in hollow trees in fairly open country, tawny owls in forests and parks, and the long-eared owl in old nests in the forest.

When they are fully grown, birds of the three larger breeds of owl are put into fairly spacious aviaries, which should be roughly 4 yd. long and 80 in. in height and width. Owls will thrive there and will live together peacefully, as long as they have enough to eat. If we ever forget to feed them, they may easily kill each other. Little owls need less space. An aviary measuring $80 \times 60 \times 72$ in. is large enough for them. Individual birds can also be kept indoors in cages as small as $60 \times 40 \times 40$ in.

Sometimes it is necessary to dispose of the birds. Good homes must be found for them, or we must make sure that they will get used to freedom, although this is only likely to happen in the case of the kestrel. At first, feed the bird almost entirely on dead mice and sparrows, leave the door of its cage open and place some food on the roof. The birds generally stay in the district for some time and collect their food in the accustomed spots. Usually, tragedy results and the much-loved kestrel is shot by a gamekeeper. Owls, fed on butcher's meat from their earliest days, are quite unable to get their own food and would starve to death if they had to fend for themselves. We should therefore remember our responsibility towards them and find them a new home, perhaps with another bird-lover or at a zoo.

Swans, geese, ducks and other aquatic birds, have been kept in captivity since time immemorial. To have a pond with an active bird-life in the garden may seem a little ambitious at first. But it is not too difficult, particularly since many birds only need a few square yards of water, where they may even breed.

It is, of course, absolutely essential to keep out all predators. Foxes, martens, weasels and stoats are no great menace in most places. But stray dogs and cats are just as dangerous and must be carefully guarded against. Although at night most waterfowl take refuge on the water—where they are beyond the reach of their enemies, if the pond or lake is big enough—they love promenading on solid ground during the day, when they are at the mercy of their enemies. The females, especially, are in great danger when they are sitting tightly on their nests near the shore.

How do we build a pool, or dam a stream? This is largely a matter of price and locality. It is not enough to have a pool near a lawn. An inlet and an outlet must be arranged. A pond must be cleaned from time to time, if it is not to get too dirty and smelly. It is, of course, simplest if there is a stream or spring nearby, which can be dammed and thus transformed into a pond. There would then be a steady supply of fresh water, and no worries about maintenance and expense. Find out, however, if the local by-laws allow a stream to be dammed. Assuming that they do, the dam can be built by oneself or left to an expert. The concrete dam—two thick planks have been inserted to hold back the water—shown in the illustration is not too difficult or expensive to make. It must be remembered that ducks and geese love to congregate near the bank, which slowly recedes as a result. The pond very gradually increases its area but gets shallower. We can prevent this by lining the edge with concrete, brick or stone. At the same time, the water must be very shallow near the edge, and the sides of the pool must slope very gradually to allow the birds to land without difficulty. Waterfowl can drown just as easily as other birds, if they have had no opportunity for bathing for some time as a result of a lengthy journey or from frost. The plumage is no longer impervious to water, the bird gets wet, panics, and is dragged down by its own weight. The pool must therefore

How to dam a stream. A simple weir

have enough landing places within easy access of even a frightened and exhausted bird.

If there is no natural source of water the pond must be constructed. Fresh water is either obtained from the mains or by tapping the water table, i.e. the subterranean springs that feed our rivers. Both methods need the permission of the local authority. Electric pumps are obviously preferable to hand pumps. An artificial pond also needs an outlet. This can either be linked to the main sewer or the water can run towards a

lawn or into a soak-away pit. There must be a certain amount
of fall in the ground if the first solution is adopted. Finally, a
pump can also be used to empty the pool. The illustration on
p. 197 shows a possible type of outlet. There are two layers of
boards—instead of one, as shown in p. 196—with a gap not
less than the width of a spade between them. The boards are
held in position by pieces of U-shaped angle iron, which have
been set into the concrete. Before filling the pond, fill the gap
between the boards with earth until no water can possibly
escape. When draining the pond, first remove the earth and
then the boards.

A love of birds, even of waterfowl, does not necessarily go
with a talent for building construction. Is there really any need
to stress how much
damage can be done
by the unskilled
building enthusiast?
Unless, therefore, we
are quite sure of
what we are doing,
and, preferably, have
done it before, we
should not venture
into building our
own pool.

The simplest type of lock

Only very large ponds do not have to be emptied regularly,
but even the fortunate owner of a large pool should beware of
having too many birds, who would only cause dirt. Depth will
depend on the size of the birds, but, in any case, need never
be more than 40 in. Remains of food, dead leaves, etc., are
quickly destroyed by water snails, frogs, etc., down to that
level, and would merely accumulate and rot in greater depths.
Having dug the pond and raised its sides (if it is to be slightly
above ground level) line it to avoid loss of water. Only pools on
a non-porous clay subsoil need no lining, although sand and
clay become water-proof after some time if enough birds are
kept, whose droppings will encourage the growth of algae,
which the water sucks to the sides, eventually sealing them and

Black Stork, *Ciconia nigra.* 40 in. Europe to Mongolia and China. **White Stork,** *Ciconia ciconia.* 42 in. Europe to Turkestan, northwest Africa. **Heron,** *Ardea cinerea.* 32 in. British Isles, Europe, Asia, Africa. The far smaller Night Heron, *Nycticorax nycticorax.* 24½ in., occurs throughout all four continents and presents no special problems in captivity. The adult bird is black above, with grey wings, pale below, and has long, drooping white feathers at the neck. **Coot,** *Fulica atra.* 15 in. British Isles, Europe, Asia, northwest Africa. Several varieties. **Purple Gallinule,** *Porphyrio porphyrio.* 19 in. Spain, Portugal, North Africa to India and Australia. Many varieties. The bird in the illustration comes from the Mediterranean. **Moorhen,** *Gallinula chloropus.* 13 in. Europe, Asia, Africa. Several varieties.

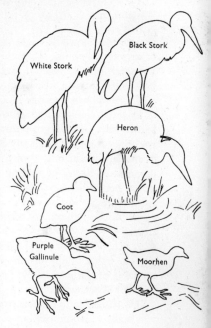

making them water-proof. But a lot of water will be used before this happens. Gravel always lets water through, and ponds on a gravel subsoil will therefore need a layer of concrete at the bottom. A layer of concrete between three and five inches thick, rendered with a ¾-in. layer of water-proof cement, is the most effective, but also the most expensive, method. It is often sufficient to concrete merely the bottom of the pool to a thickness of one or two inches, and to strengthen only the frost-endangered sides. Such a thin shell will acquire a few cracks in the course of time, but these will soon be closed by the accumulated droppings of the birds. The banks must be very shallow and the sides must rise very gradually if concrete is used, because snow and ice will do the greatest damage at the water's edge. The pool, of course, will be deepest in the middle, whence a pipe will lead to the outlet. A five-inch layer of potter's clay or loam can be used in place of concrete. It must be thoroughly damped and rammed in. The edges must also be reinforced with brick or concrete, because the pond would otherwise spread and the water silt up. It does not matter if the clay shows cracks even before the pond is filled. An outlet is also needed with a pipe and some fall in ground. Plants with strong roots, like rushes or calamus, must not be allowed in a pond with a clay bottom, because they would grow through the clay and thus cause the water to disappear gradually into the soil. But if there are many birds, any plants will probably get eaten before they do any damage. A lining of roofing felt, each sheet being carefully tarred before the next layer is applied, is quite adequate, if the sides of the pond rise very gradually towards a clearly outlined edge. Finally, there are various plastics and rubber-backed adhesive materials which can be used as a lining and covered with a thick layer of sand. Algae and birds' droppings will close any tears that might develop in the course of time. As always, the edge of the pool has to be reinforced with stone, concrete, brick or sheet metal.

It is advisable to have several small islands in the pool. These will make welcome nesting places for ducks, geese and swans.

A wide stretch of lawn is essential near ponds, especially for geese, to whom lettuce and other green stuff are only a poor substitute for their natural food, grass. Swans also like to graze, if there is not an abundance of aquatic plants. Many ducks also enjoy it and will also search enthusiastically for earthworms. These, and small insects, etc., form an important part of their diet.

Pond and lawn will have to be surrounded with a 24 to 28 in. high fence to prevent the geese and ducks from running away. Newcomers, particularly, will try desperately to escape while their surroundings are still strange to them. They will look for opportunities everywhere, will explore the fence for holes and may easily suffer injury or starve as a result. Once acclimatised, however, they take to the water when they feel themselves in danger.

Several feeding places will be needed, depending on the number of birds kept. If the pond is large, and there are many birds, floats will be the best solution. These are simply made of two carefully sealed, water-tight oil barrels and a large detachable low-rimmed tray, with a ledge all round, where the birds can stand comfortably when they want to feed. The float is moored close to the edge of the pool. To refill it, simply pull it ashore, take off the tray, clean it thoroughly, fill it, replace it, and push the float back. The birds take up their position on the float, dipping their bills alternately into their food and into the water, as they love doing. If the pond is very small, place bowls, containing two compartments, one for water and one for food, on the shore. Wooden trays, without floats—also on the shore and close to the water—from which

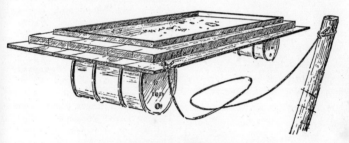

A float with detachable feeding tray

the birds can take their food without coming on land, are alternatives. Cleanliness is most important when using this method, because left-overs soon rot, smell badly and are harmful to the birds.

Now for the food itself. An excellent mixture can be made from five parts mashed potato, three parts soaked bread, two parts wheat bran, two parts barley meal, two parts maize meal, and one part fish meal or meat meal. This is mixed very thoroughly and enriched with calcium food, grit and charcoal. Add, also, grass seed, obtained by sweeping a near-empty hayloft, and, in winter, one part boiled and mashed carrot.

If the lawn is very large, the birds will be able to find their own green and live food, and the mixture can be kept much simpler in consequence. Soaked bread, fish or meat meal and green food will be omitted. The pond itself—provided it is

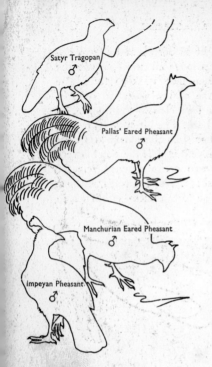

Satyr Tragopan, *Tragopan satyrus.* 22 in. The female dark brown above, with black and light brown patches on the back; lighter below, with large white spots. Himalayas to Gharwal and Assam. Blyth's Tragopan, *Tragopan blythi*, has a yellow, instead of a blue, patch of skin near the face, and grey underparts tipped with brown. Assam and Burma. Temminck's Tragopan, *Tragopan temmincki*, has grey, instead of white, spots below. Frontier zone of Tibet, from Annam to Shensi and Hupei, Yünnan and Szechwan. **Pallas' Eared Pheasant,** *Crossoptilon auritum.* 40 in. The female without spurs. Kansu, central China. **Manchurian Eared Pheasant,** *Crossoptilon manchuricum.* 40 in. The female without spurs. Shansi and Chihli (northern China). The Tibetan Eared Pheasant is white and has no whiskers. **Impeyan Pheasant,** *Lophophorus impeyanus.* 28 in. The female has a white throat and a smaller crest, and is dark brown, with lighter and darker patches above, light brown, tipped darker, below. Himalayas to Afghanistan and Bhutan.

---

fairly large—also supplies a lot of food for swans and ducks. The swans eat aquatic plants, and the divers, such as the rosy-billed duck or the red-crested pochard, hunt for small fishes, insects, snails and similar creatures at the bottom.

If the pond should freeze during the winter, the birds must be brought into a shed, deeply littered with straw, which must be replaced frequently. Their food is given to them in bowls, care being taken always to place a bowl of food next to a bowl of water. The birds' diet will have to be much more varied than in the open.

The area of water needed by each species differs greatly.

Black-winged Peafowl. A variant of the Common Peafowl. The female almost white, with brown and grey patches. **Common Peafowl,** *Pavo cristatus.* The male, with train, over 80 in.; the female, without train, inconspicuously coloured, with a smaller crest. Head, neck and back dark brown, shot with green; throat white, lower neck and breast metallic green, with light tips, otherwise shades of brown above and buff-white below. India and Ceylon. A white and a pied variant also occur. **Green Peafowl,** *Pavo muticus.* The male, with train, up to 92 in., the female similar, but duller and with shorter tail. Southern India to Siam and Java. Hybrids between the Common and the Green Peafowl appear occasionally on the market. They resemble both parents. Although much hardier than the Green Peafowl, they command a lower price.

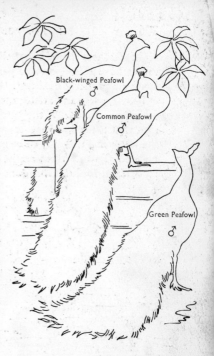

Smaller ducks, like mandarin duck and wood duck, will be content with less than 3 sq. yd. per head; a pair of swans must have least 250 sq. yd. A pond of a fifth of an acre will accommodate 50 different ducks, 10 to 15 geese and a few swans. Geese, as already mentioned, need water less than a lawn. Ducks are usually peaceful. Occasional fights very rarely lead to serious casualties. Geese, by contrast, become very aggressive towards their own kind during the breeding season once they have paired. The Egyptian goose, Canada goose and the different varieties of shelduck will attack any goose and even large ducks. No pond will hold more than one pair of swans.

Birds should only be bought from reputable firms. Each bird should be immediately examined for a plump rounded breast and for any possible defects. It is most important to ensure that the wings have been pinioned. If only the primaries or flight feathers have been clipped, pinion immediately, or rather have this operation performed as soon as possible by someone properly qualified. Only one wing is pinioned.

Ducks, geese and swans, etc., are almost impossible to catch otherwise. Normally, the birds' successful escape is the only sign that the wings have grown again. Ducks will race across the water and will only be caught when they are completely exhausted. To trap them easily, a special cage, well stocked with food, should be built above one of the birds' usual feeding places.

Open-fronted box, converted into a duck's nest, and camouflaged with twigs

Pinioning immediately after arrival, when the birds are exhausted from the journey, involves a certain risk. It is therefore all the more important that it should be entrusted to an expert.

Newcomers must be watched very carefully when they take to the water for the first time. Their plumage might be wet, and there might be difficulties with old-established residents. If the bird gets soaked, catch it at once and put it into a shed, where it is given a large trough or tin bath so as to get gradually used to water again. Only frequent bathing will make its plumage water-proof. Ducks take some time to acclimatise themselves; geese and swans recover somewhat faster.

Geese and swans travel in large round baskets, smaller geese and ducks in chip baskets of the type used for mushrooms, tomatoes, etc. All baskets are covered with sacking, which is sewn carefully to the edges. Birds should never have to travel for more than a day. If they have a good feed before they are sent off, they will not need any more until they arrive.

There should be as many nesting facilities as possible near the pond. For the ducks, place fir twigs along the banks to form shelters accessible from the water. Open-fronted wooden boxes, facing the water, are another solution. Simply scratch a hollow in the sheltered portion, and cover the box with fir twigs, only allowing a small opening to show. Finally, there are the so-called Berlin nests, consisting of small boards—rather like a seed box without a bottom—to which fir twigs are nailed, also leaving only a small opening facing the water. Most ducks accept such nests enthusiastically; only wood duck and mandarin duck breed in hollows (see

A Berlin nest

p. 217). Shelducks and Egyptian geese also like to use nest boxes; other geese are not so anxious to hide their eggs and prefer to lay on small islands. The gander stands on guard next to his mate and defends the nest with her. Swans like to nest surrounded by water. Therefore place a stone-filled barrel or box, or a concrete ring, in the pond, allowing only the top to show very slightly, so that it is still touched by water. This platform—on which the swans will build their nest—should have a diameter of between 2 ft. and 2 ft. 6 in., or can be 2 ft. square. It must be sufficiently far from the shore to give the birds protection—preferably not less than 16–20 ft. Then cover it with grass turves to a height of approximately 8 in. If rushes and straw are thrown on the water, the birds will collect these materials and build their nest from them.

Duck nests must be controlled daily. The first egg is replaced by a plaster egg, to which several others are added later.

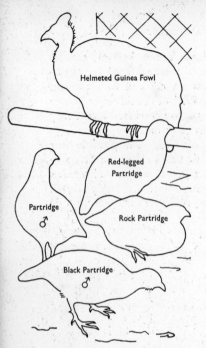

Helmeted Guinea Fowl

Red-legged Partridge

Partridge ♂

Rock Partridge

Black Partridge ♂

Helmeted Guinea Fowl, *Numida meleagris*. 22 in. East Africa. There are many varieties of Guinea Fowl, including several species of the Tufted Guinea fowl, *Numida meleagris mitrata*, from East Africa. **Red-legged Partridge,** *Alectoris rufa*. 13 in. British Isles, western Europe to Azores and Canary Isles. **Rock Partridge,** *Alectoris graeca*. 13½ in. From the Alps and Italy to Manchuria and northern India. The bird in the illustration is the European variety, *Alectoris graeca saxatilis*. It is not unlike the Chukor, *Alectoris graeca Chukar*, from northern India, except that the Chukor has a yellowish patch on the throat and a rust-red, instead of a black, band round the face. **Black Partridge,** *Francolinus francolinus*. 13¼ in. The female lighter, with yellowish-white throat, underparts almost black, with lighter bars. From Cyprus and Asia Minor to Assam. Many other varieties, usually less conspicuously coloured, occur in Africa, some also in southern Asia. **Partridge,** *Perdix perdix*. 10 in. In the female, the brown patch on the belly is smaller or missing altogether. British Isles, Europe, western Asia.

Crows and other predators cannot harm plaster eggs, and they must be forestalled, since ducks do not defend their eggs—which are mostly laid early in the morning—but spend the day roaming around. When the clutch is complete, the female duck pulls out some of her breast feathers. This is a sure sign that incubation is about to start. The plaster eggs can now be removed and the duck's own eggs returned, unless these are entrusted to turkeys or domestic hens, who will also act as foster-parents. If ducks are left to rear their young, there are usually many losses, although these can be avoided to some extent if mother and offspring are put into a small enclosure

California Quail, *Lophortyx californica.* 9½ in. The female has a shorter crest and no black markings on head and throat, which are greyish-brown, flecked white. Western U.S.A. to California. **Virginia Partridge,** *Colinus virginianus.* 9 in. The head of the female yellowish-brown, without any black. U.S.A. to northern Mexico. The Virginia Partridge and the California Quail are bred on a large scale in the U.S.A. and can be obtained in Europe without difficulty. **Dwarf Quail,** *Coturnix chinensis.* Also called Chinese Painted Quail. 5 in. The female a mottled greyish-brown above, yellowish-white underneath, with banded breast and flanks. India to southern China and Australia. A closely related type of quail also occurs in Africa. **Quail,** *Coturnix coturnix.* 8 in. The female has a lighter patch on the throat. British Isles, Europe, Asia, Africa.

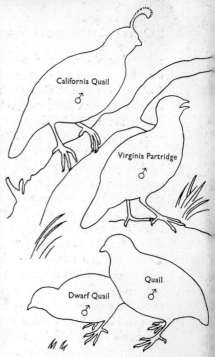

California Quail ♂

Virginia Partridge ♂

Quail ♂

Dwarf Quail ♂

---

containing a pond, immediately after hatching, and are locked in at night.

Geese are usually good breeders. Birds of strong family feeling—even the father takes his share in looking after the nest—they will rear their own brood. But here, too, catch the whole family and put them into a small enclosure, as in the case of ducks. This will make some extra feeding necessary, but it is well worth it, not least because shelducks and Egyptian geese will attack everything that comes within reach of their young.

Rearing enclosures are simply patches of lawn, fenced with wire-netting to a height of 20 to 24 in. A large box—covered with a tarpaulin during the night—will serve as sleeping quarters. The food for the ducklings, or goslings, is kept under a bell-shaped cage, with bars sufficiently wide apart to admit the young, but not their parents. The rearing food for the first few days consists of chopped hard-boiled egg, soaked bread-crumbs, flaked wheat, ants' eggs and, above all, duckweed. If this is not available, chopped dandelions, lettuce and young stinging nettles can be given instead. The enclosure, complete with basin, is moved every few days so that the birds do not have to graze on stale soil. This is particularly important in the case of the larger ducks, whose young should be accustomed to picking their own grass as soon as possible. Goslings and ducklings soon start to eat the same food as their parents. If there is a pond nearby, duckweed—which should be fresh daily—can be obtained from it. Duckweed is not only a wholesome green food, but also contains many small algae, which are eagerly devoured by the ducks.

Young swans must have water. Their legs are not sufficiently strong to support their heavy bodies on land for any length of time and their bones would sooner or later become deformed. Swans are even more devoted to each other than geese and will defend their young fiercely. They should therefore never be hand-reared. The parents hatch and rear their own families. A special rearing food—apart from extra green food, which is cut up and thrown to the birds on the water—is unnecessary.

The young of all waterfowl can be pinioned as soon as they are hatched, when they are easily caught. Otherwise, their flight feathers must be clipped frequently, taking care not to hurt the quills, which contain the blood vessels. When catching a bird for pinioning, avoid any prolonged or undue chase. Pinioning, while the flight feathers are still growing, causes considerable loss of blood and is therefore dangerous. Young swans usually cannot be pinioned until they have reached a certain age, since they are very attached to their parents and do not leave them, unless they are really frightened.

Pinioning, needless to say, is an unpleasant operation. Whenever possible, it should be avoided. Many English authorities consider it unnecessary in the case of the more sedentary breeds, such as Carolina ducks, mandarin ducks, tree ducks, etc., provided the birds are kept in a sufficiently large enclosure. Undoubtedly, ducks are far more interesting, give more pleasure and breed more readily, if they are kept fully winged. We must again stress that one wing only is pinioned and that to pinion both would be utterly senseless cruelty.

It is obviously essential for breeding to have properly matched pairs. Amongst ducks, male and female are, as a rule, very different in breeding dress; where there is no special breeding dress—as, for example, in the case of Bahama duck, Chiloe widgeon and yellow-billed duck—the drakes are brighter throughout the year. In the summer, the colour of the bill is usually a safe guide. Amongst geese and swans, the plumage of both sexes is alike. The males, however, behave rather aggressively during the breeding season, when they attack every real or imaginary enemy. For the rest of the year, the sexes are very much alike. Although the males of aquatic birds have a strongly developed reproductive organ, this only projects during mating. It is therefore best to have a written guarantee from the vendor, stating that the birds would be exchanged if they should turn out to be of the same sex.

A pair of swans needs at least 250 sq. yd. of water for breeding; a pair of ducks will be content with little more than a small garden pool. The rather goose-like shelduck also needs water, while geese are more interested in lawns. But if geese are to breed, they should have a few square yards of fairly deep water, since they will as a rule only mate while swimming.

Young geese and ducks are easily reared in brooders. Amongst ducks, birds of the same brood stick together, are happy in each other's company and readily accept the rearing lamp—which can be bought at most pet shops—as the source of all comfort. Geese feel lonely without a mother, or foster-mother, whom they can follow during the first few weeks. Domestic hens, turkey hens and Muscovy ducks will readily oblige. It is important to know the lengths of the

Herring Gull, *Larus argentatus.* 22½ in. British Isles, Europe. **Great Black-backed Gull,** *Larus marinus.* 29½ in. British Isles, Europe, northern Asia, Greenland. **White Pelican,** *Pelecanus onocrotalus.* 64 in. South-eastern Europe to China, south-east Asia (occasional vagrant only) and South Africa. **Dalmatian Pelican,** *Pelecanus crispus.* 64 in. From south-eastern Europe to central Asia and northern China. **Humboldt's Penguin,** *Spheniscus humboldti.* 26 in. Coasts of Peru, northern Chile. **Jackass Penguin,** *Spheniscus demersus.* 24 in. Coastal areas of South Africa. The Magellan Penguin, *Spheniscus magellanicus.* 24 in., from the coastal regions of the Argentine and northern Chile, has two bands across the breast. The Antarctic penguins, especially the King Penguin, *Aptenodytes patachonica,* 40 in., do very badly in captivity. They soon succumb to warm weather and die.

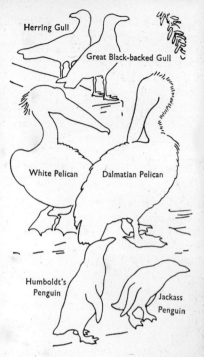

incubating periods and these are given below for the following species:

Black swan	*c.* 40 days
Mute swan	36 days
Grey Lag goose	28 days
Shelduck (most varieties)	29 days
Domestic duck	28 days
Mallard	26 days
Red-crested pochard	28 days
Wood duck, or bridal duck	31 days
Mandarin duck	31 days
Muscovy duck	35 days

If the eggs of different breeds are to be hatched by the same bird, start her off with eggs that take longer, adding the others as necessary. Domestic hens take 21 days, and turkey hens 28,

Whooper Swan, *Cygnus cygnus.*
60 in. British Isles (winter visitor),
northern Europe, northern Asia.
The very similar Bewick's Swan,
Cygnus bewickii, 49 in., has more
black, and less yellow, on the bill.
Also a winter visitor, more com-
mon in Scotland, otherwise nor-
thern Europe and Asia. **Mute
Swan,** *Cygnus olor.* 60 in. British
Isles, Europe to China and Japan.
Black Swan, *Cygnus atratus.*
44 in. Australia. **White-fronted
Goose,** *Anser albifrons.* 32 in.
Arctic Europe, Asia, North Ame-
rica. **Bean Goose,** *Anser ar-
vensis,* also called *A. fabalis.* 32 in.
Northern Europe, northern Asia.
The similar Pink-footed Goose,
Anser brachyrhynchus, 28 in., from
Greenland, Iceland and Spitz-
bergen, and a winter visitor to the
British Isles, has pink feet and is
pink, instead of yellow, at the base
of the bill. **Grey Lag Goose**
Anser anser. 32 in. Europe, northern and central Asia. Several
varieties.

to hatch their own eggs, although both will generally stay on
their nest long enough to hatch the eggs of other breeds.

When the ducklings are hatched, make sure that the hen
accepts them as her own and does not chase them away or hurt
them. The ducklings, too, will have to get used to their foster-
mother. To hasten this process, the whole family is at first kept
in a small enclosure. Food and water are placed directly against
the nest, dried ants' eggs are thrown on the water to keep the
ducklings from starving until they can recognise other food.
During that time—usually three or four days—the foster-
mother comes to accept these odd, squeaking creatures as hers,
and they, in turn, also learn the meaning of her calls.

Breeds nesting in hollows, like mandarin and wood ducks,
are kept exactly like other aquatic birds, unless they are required to breed, which is rather difficult in a pond. Kept in

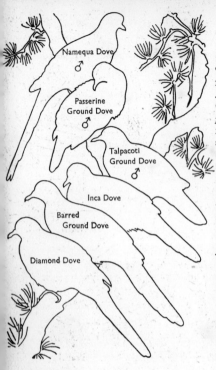

Namequa Dove, *Oena capensis*. 9½ in. Female has white chin and forehead and brownish throat. Africa, Madagascar. **Passerine Ground Dove**, *Columbigallina passerina*. 6½ in. The female less ruddy and more grey. Southern states of U.S.A. to Guatemala. Several varieties. **Talpacoti Ground Dove**, *Columbigallina talpacoti*. 7½ in. The female duller. Columbia and Guiana to northern Argentine and Paraguay. **Inca Dove**, *Scardafella inca*. 8½ in. California, central America. The very similar Scaled Dove, *Scardafella squammata*, Columbia to Brazil, has dark bars across the breast. **Barred Ground Dove**, *Geopelia striata*. 9 in. Southern India, Malay Peninsula, Philippines. **Diamond Dove**, *Geopelia cuneata*. 8 in. Australia. No cage or aviary should contain more than one pair of the two last-named doves, because they are apt to fight and disturb each other.

large numbers, they may do so, but it is not very common even then. To breed regularly, both species should be kept in aviaries with small pools, each enclosure containing only one pair. Such an aviary should be 80 in. high and extend over a minimum area of 8 sq. yd., a third of which should be taken up by water. Back and sides are boarded up to give cover and protection against frost, and a few strong branches are fitted horizontally, so that the birds can roost as fully winged specimens love to do. Finally, fit nest-boxes; these must have an inlet of 5 in. diameter, and inner measurements of 10 in. × 10 in. × 16 in. At the beginning of April, everything is made ready and the birds are placed in the aviary. Let the ducks take charge of their own young, although the drake must be removed as soon as the duck has seriously settled on her nest.

Wood Pigeon, or **Ring Dove**, *Columba palumbus*. 17 in. British Isles, Europe, western Asia, North Africa. Several varieties. **Stock Dove**, *Columba oenas*. 13 in. British Isles, Europe, North Africa, western Asia. Stock Dove and Wood Pigeon will cross with domestic pigeons. **Tambourine Dove**, *Tympanistria tympanistria*. 9 in. The female smaller and duller. Africa, south of the Sahara, Madagascar. **Little Brown Dove**, *Streptopelia senegalensis*. 11 in. Africa, western Asia to India. **Bleeding Heart Dove**, *Gallicolumba luzonica*. 10 in. Luzon (Philippines). Bartlett's Bleeding Heart Dove, *Gallicolumba crinigera*, of Mindanao, is much darker. **Pink-headed Dove**, *Streptopelia decaocto roseigrisea*. 12 in. A domestic breed of the north-east African form of the Collared Turtledove. Many sports have been produced by breeders, amongst them a white bird, which, however, is rather sensitive to cold.

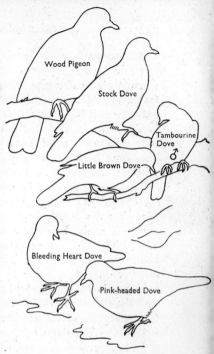

The water must be changed frequently, especially after the eggs have hatched.

The following birds are hardy and can be highly recommended for ponds of all descriptions:

Ducks	*Geese*	*Swans*
Mandarin duck	Egyptian goose	Mute swan
Wood duck, or bridal duck	Shelduck	Whooper swan
Pintail	Ruddy shelduck	Black swan
Yellow-billed duck	Canada goose	
Chiloe widgeon	Barnacle goose	
Spotbill	Bean goose	
Baikal teal	Grey Lag goose	
Teal (European variety)	White-fronted goose	
Rosy-billed duck		
Red-crested pochard		

Bahama duck, blue-winged and cinnamon teal, and white-faced duck are sensitive to cold and should be kept in a shed where their drinking water cannot freeze during prolonged frosts. The Muscovy duck, from South America, is also visibly unhappy if it has to spend day and night in the open during hard winters. Rosy-billed duck and red-crested pochard are diving ducks and must have a pond at least 2 ft. deep. All these handsome birds are readily available and present no great problems in captivity.

Ducks can be joined by crakes, rails and coots. Coots and moorhens, both hardy indigenous birds, breed frequently in captivity; the handsome purple gallinule, from the tropics, only very rarely. When hand-rearing, remember that rails and allied birds—like cranes—dangle the food for their offspring before them in their bills. The young will therefore starve to death if some food is merely put down in a bowl, or if they are left to be brought up by hens and turkeys, neither of which feed their chicks in this manner. It is necessary, therefore, to take the place of the mother ourselves, by using a pair of tweezers to feed them.

Red and pink flamingoes, with their webbed feet, long necks and curved bills, are a magnificent sight. In contrast to all other birds, they have also a jointed upper mandible. Flamingoes are good swimmers, make trumpeting sounds, and have a remarkable social life. In winter, they have to be kept in a shed in which the temperature must not fall below 50 deg. F. (10 deg. C.). Such a shed must contain a small pond, where they can bathe and wade about. The water must be renewed very frequently to ensure the utmost cleanliness. A shed covering an area of 8 sq. yd. will be sufficient for six flamingoes. The floor should be covered with sand or, better still, asphalt, which is easily cleaned and is not as hard as concrete. In summer, the flamingoes wade elegantly along the shore of the pond, uttering their melodious and not so melodious calls. Their food is put into buckets, which are stood in the pond. Like ducks, flamingoes eat and drink alternately. A good flamingo mixture can be made up from 1 lb. of shrimps, $\frac{1}{2}$ lb. of boiled rice, 2 lb. of wheat, $\frac{1}{2}$ lb. of crushed hemp and 2 lb. of mashed potato. This can be enriched with 2 lb. of lean, minced meat. Everything is mixed thoroughly and moistened. In winter, add finely chopped boiled carrots; in summer, flamingoes should have as many daphniae (water fleas) as can be caught for them with fine gauze nets in village ponds, etc., if there are none in their own pond. The more daphniae they can be given, the better they will keep their red colour, which is absorbed through the red water fleas and deposited in the feathers. Daphniae are rich in this particular substance and are also very good for flamingoes. Unfortunately, flamingoes have not bred in captivity up to now. Until they are used to their new surroundings, their enclosure should be fenced in to a height of not less than 5 ft. 6 in. to prevent their escape; once they are settled, this can be reduced to 28 in.

Herons and storks settle happily with fully grown ducks and geese, but will eat newly hatched ducklings and goslings, which must therefore be kept out of their reach. Herons, in particular, are very keen on chicks of every kind. Both storks and herons must be pinioned or have their wings clipped. They have to be kept safely fenced in—to a minimum height of 5 ft. 6 in.— because herons, especially, peck at the eyes of anyone standing close to them. Once escaped, they are a great menace, and must therefore be guarded very carefully.

Herons and storks are fed with raw meat and cheap offal. From time to time, they need the cheaper kinds of fish, used normally only as bait. Herons can stand any temperature; storks should be kept in frost-proof sheds, with the floor covered with chaff or saw-dust during the winter. Storks need deep drinking vessels, in which they can submerge their long bills completely. If they are required to breed readily, the birds must have far more fish. The young storks will have hatched after 30 days and the young herons after 25 days. They should be reared on very small fishes. Herons, white stork and black stork are frequently offered for sale and, properly cared for, live for many years.

Pelicans and sea-gulls will thrive on a similar diet consisting chiefly of meat, with an occasional fish. Both are dangerous to smaller ducks—especially to the young—and should therefore have a pond of their own. Our larger indigenous gulls, the great black-backed gull and the herring gull, are extremely hardy; pelicans are tropical and sub-tropical birds and need some kind of frost-proof shelter with adequate bathing facilities; an area of 1 sq. yd. per bird is considered sufficient, and the basin should be at least 16 in. deep. The shed should have a concrete, or preferably asphalt, floor.

Dalmatian and white pelicans are offered for sale fairly frequently. Both can be fed with bits of absolutely fresh, raw fish. A steady supply of salt-water fish is, fortunately, no problem in the British Isles. Some fishmongers supply special coarse fish—given mostly to cats—which will also do for pelicans, so long as it is really fresh. This cannot be stressed sufficiently.

Herring gulls and great black-backed gulls will breed readily, if their fish and meat diet is made a little more interesting with bread, cut-up mice, dead sparrows and crushed sea-shells.

Fresh salt-water fish is absolutely essential for penguins. These charming birds come from the Southern Hemisphere; several varieties, amongst them the jackass penguin from South Africa, and Humboldt's penguin from South America, venture very far north along their native shores and can therefore stand our climate fairly well. They are best kept on their own. A 2-ft. deep pool, covering an area of from 6 to 8 sq. yd., will be sufficient for three or four penguins. The water must be fairly deep to allow the birds to dive properly, and should be renewed very frequently. A continuous flow of fresh water is even better. Both the jackass penguin and Humboldt's penguin do well in captivity, as long as each bird gets about 1 lb. of absolutely fresh fish per day. They will even breed, if they have open-fronted boxes to nest in. The clutch is small—it consists of only one or two eggs—and the incubating period lasts 38 days. The penguin pool should be surrounded with a 2-ft. high fence, constructed in such a way that the birds cannot slip through underneath. Like geese, penguins love to strut around and need long runs or paddocks.

PARK BIRDS

Many animal-lovers dream of a park, or even garden, where peacocks and pheasants move about at complete liberty. Such a dream will not materialise without difficulty. If the birds are to move about freely, they must be protected against all predators, especially foxes. The park will therefore have to be within a fairly built-up area, or surrounded by a high wall or a combination of low wall and high wire fence. A wall would have to be at least 7 ft. high, a fence even higher, to prevent the foxes from scaling it or jumping across.

Birds will not harm lawns or luxuriant perennials, but are very hard on vegetable gardens and carpet bedding.

The common peafowl, in all its varieties, is the most popular park bird. It needs no great attention. A feeding place should be provided—with a low roof to protect the food from the weather—where the birds are fed twice, or preferably three times, daily, to prevent them from straying too far afield. New birds should be kept in a provisional enclosure, where they can get used to their new setting and study it at first through the wire mesh. Before they are let out—after about a fortnight, or later—they should have the flight feathers of one wing clipped. They will then only be fully winged after the next moult. Until then, they must be kept in a shed at night. Their wings having grown again, they will explore further afield and will roost at night, in the manner of all healthy and fully winged peacocks. The sturdy branches of their choice are high up, well beyond the reach of an enemy. This sets something of a problem: if the park or garden is not too extensive, clip the wings of the peacocks, or they might do serious damage to the garden of a neighbour; but this keeps them from roosting and thus exposes them to greater danger from foxes, unless a wall or fence has been built all round. Peahens are in special danger: they nest on the ground, where they cannot be seen and where the fox can easily get at them. A few bloodstained feathers are often the only proof that there has been a nest. Hens should therefore be kept in an enclosure during the nesting season. As soon as the young leave their nest, the hen should have one of her wings clipped and be allowed to roam with her young. She must, of course, be kept in a safe place at night.

Peafowl generally do not live very long in the colder parts of Europe, at least not as long as in friendlier climates. They suffer badly in very cold winters and frequently become the victims of tuberculosis. This applies particularly to fully grown males, to whom the annual moult is always a great strain. Frost-proof sleeping places are therefore very important.

Every mature peacock needs a fairly large territory—where he will not tolerate any other males. If more than one cock is to be kept, at least $2\frac{1}{2}$ acres are necessary. Each peacock should have from two to four hens who will seek him during the mating season, but will otherwise show no interest in him. The first clutch should be given to a turkey hen, but care should be taken that it does not get mixed up with the prospective foster-mother's own eggs. Some turkey hens will recognise the strangers amongst their own brood and peck them to death, though they are quite ready to accept them if no turkey chicks are present. The second clutch follows the first after a short interval and is hatched by the real mother. The incubating period lasts 28 days, as it does in the case of turkeys. It is best to give the young peafowl and their mother the freedom of the garden in fine weather, taking care at the same time to feed them very frequently. When it is cold or damp, they must be kept in a dry shed, since they can stand rain and dew no better than turkey chicks. If they are to be reared in a coop, this must be moved as often as possible, because the young birds may suffer very badly if they have to stand in their own droppings. Broody domestic hens can also be used as foster-mothers, although they are not as satisfactory as turkey hens. Dry, warm, sunny weather is the most important element in rearing peafowl chicks—which grow very slowly—during the first few weeks of their lives.

There are several varieties of the common peafowl: feral (called blue), white, pied and black-shouldered. The cock of the last-named variety has black wings, and is thus much darker than his blue cousin; the hen, however, is very much lighter—indeed almost white—than the female of the original species. Black-winged and white peacocks command higher prices than other birds. The cock is not in full breeding dress until his third year, when he develops his train, which is not formed by the tail-feathers, but by the upper tail coverts. He will also have reached maturity by then, although hens may already breed in their second year. Young peafowl are not too easily sexed: young birds also spread their trains, even hens. Mature hens also sometimes behave like males; a peafowl in non-breeding dress at display is therefore not necessarily a cock. The safest guide to the sex of the young common peafowl are the primaries which are already yellowish-brown in the male and grey-brown in the female in the first autumn.

Another species, the green peafowl, from southern India, is not nearly as hardy as its northern relation and needs a heated, and not merely frost-proof, shed in winter. It is given the same food as the other varieties, with which it will cross readily, producing rather attractive offspring. Peafowl do not settle down well to cage life and require a lot of attention, unless they are kept at liberty in large parks, where they can, at their own leisure, supplement with insects and green food, etc., the food given them by their owners.

Where peafowl and turkeys are kept together, the cocks are apt to fight each other, particularly if the peafowl were reared by turkey hens and have therefore come to look on turkey cocks as rivals. The far more agile peacock is usually victorious in such battles.

Peacocks in non-breeding dress are easily transported; they can travel in an ordinary basket or in a box. A mature cock with a long train must be put into a long, low and narrow container, where he cannot turn and where his train can be accommodated. For a short journey, he can be put in a loosely-tied sack, with his train exposed.

Other gallinaceous birds can also be kept at liberty, amongst them the red jungle fowl, the ancestor of our innumerable breeds of domestic fowl. As amongst peacocks, each adult cock

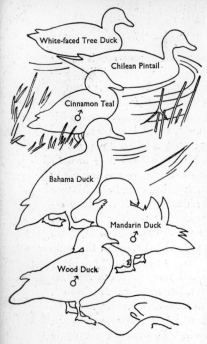

White-faced Tree Duck

Chilean Pintail

Cinnamon Teal ♂

Bahama Duck

Mandarin Duck ♂

Wood Duck ♂

White-faced Tree Duck, *Dendrocygna viduata*. 18 in. Tropical South America and Africa. **Chilean Pintail,** *Anas spinicauda*. 20 in. The female somewhat smaller. South America. **Cinnamon Teal,** *Anas cyanoptera*. 18 in. The female is mottled greyish-brown with blue-grey wing coverts, and is very hard to distinguish from f. of the Blue-winged Teal. Southern North America to Bolivia. **Bahama Duck,** *Anas bahamensis*. 20 in. Bahamas, Antilles, to northern South America to central America. **Mandarin Duck,** *Aix galericulata*. 18 in. The female resembles f. Wood Duck, but with more grey. China, Japan. **Wood** or **Bridal Duck,** *Aix sponsa*. 18 in. The female has a ring round the eye, head grey, with a small crest, throat and belly white, flanks and breast brown, mottled yellow, back grey-brown. Southern Canada to Mexico. In non-breeding dress, males of the two last-named varieties resemble females.

has his territory where he does not tolerate other males. Hens are usually only interested in one particular cock and lay their eggs anywhere in secluded spots. It is best to have the young hatched and reared by a domestic hen. If they are hatched by their own mother, separate quarters should be provided for her. The chicks are kept in a coop for the first few days and are then reared at liberty. The incubating period lasts about 20 days.

The Author has kept golden and silver pheasants at complete liberty in a large park. The birds are accustomed to their surroundings exactly like red jungle fowl, i.e. the eggs are hatched by domestic hens and the young are left to roam with their foster-mother, having spent the first weeks in a rearing coop. The pheasants thus get used to the park and are not likely to stray beyond it, if it is really large, unless they are frightened,

Spotbill, *Anas poecilorhyncha.* 22 in. India to China. **Chiloe Widgeon,** *Anas sibilatrix.* 20 in. Southernmost South America. **Blue-winged Teal,** *Anas discors.* 16 in. The female with blue-grey flight coverts and whitish throat and breast, otherwise mottled grey-brown. North America. **Baikal Teal,** *Anas formosa.* 16 in. The female mottled greyish-brown, with white throat and white patch at base of bill, underparts white. China, Japan, Formosa. **Red-crested Pochard,** *Netta rufina.* 22 in. The female a darker greyish-brown, sides of face and throat light grey, bill grey-brown with reddish tip. Mediterranean to central Asia. The male of the Pochard, *Aythya ferina,* 18½ in., is greyish-white, with reddish head and black breast. British Isles, northern Europe, Asia. **Rosy-billed Duck,** *Netta peposaca.* 20 in. The female dark brown above, lighter below, bill almost black. Southernmost South America, especially Chile.

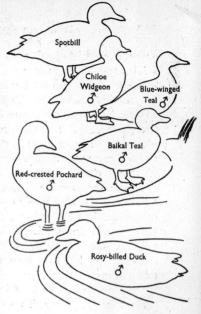

when they are apt to fly off in any direction and sometimes get lost. To prevent this, one wing can be clipped. Golden pheasants resemble peacocks in their habits, each cock having its own territory during the breeding season. Silver or Kaleege pheasants like to stay together, especially when they are still young. There is hardly a finer sight than a group of silver pheasants with the fully grown cocks in breeding dress.

The other breeds, in particular the common pheasant and Reeves' pheasant, are not suitable for keeping at liberty, because they stray very easily. Eared pheasants, or crossoptilons, are less likely to escape, if they have been reared by a domestic hen or a turkey hen. But they are expensive birds, and should therefore have one wing clipped to prevent their escape.

Magnificent parterres of carpet bedding and pheasants, or peacocks, will definitely not combine. The birds will never appreciate the labour that has gone into setting out geraniums, salvia and lobelia in neat rows. A keen bird-lover could put up with such damage to his flower beds: his neighbour may not be as friendly disposed towards pheasants and peacocks, the more so since he has probably been awakened by their raucous voices every morning for weeks past. All this can have most unpleasant consequences. It is, therefore, unfortunately necessary to keep one wing of each bird clipped, where there are comparatively close neighbours.

Cranes are quieter and less destructive, although the large-billed varieties also love to pull up an occasional plant; the others are less enthusiastic gardeners! But their truly regal bearing and attractive disposition fully compensate those people who really love these fine birds for any damage they may do. Anyone who has ever kept these handsome, lively and intelligent creatures will hardly bear to part with them.

How can cranes be kept in a park or large garden? They present few problems, if they are put in an orchard with tall trees and fairly high grass, which, however, should be mown two or three times a year to keep down stinging nettles. When this is not done, the cranes hide in the undergrowth and grow very shy.

But these waders can be kept in most gardens, as long as what little damage they may do is not resented. The garden must, of course, be carefully fenced to keep out foxes and dogs, who must not be able to jump the fence, creep through underneath, or burrow their way through to the cranes. The birds must be pinioned, or have their wings clipped (see p. 246). Since cranes stand up to pinioning very badly, many bird-lovers prefer to clip their wings. The primaries of one wing only are clipped rather short, thus causing the bird to lose its balance when it tries to fly. It must be remembered that cranes can escape even when only a few of the flight feathers have been replaced after the moult. Varieties with very broad wings, like the crowned crane, quickly gain height and are swept away by the wind. To catch them again is a very laborious task indeed.

Cranes should be locked up at night where there is any danger from foxes. They quickly get used to their shed, if they are fed there. A shed for a pair of cranes should cover at least an area of 3 sq. yd. and should be about 5 ft. 6 in. high. It only has to have solid walls on three sides to protect the birds from draughts. The front can consist of wire-netting. European cranes are absolutely hardy. The demoiselle crane, from southern Europe and southern Asia, and the crowned crane, from tropical Africa, will not stand up to the cold too well and need frost-proof accommodation, which, in the case of the crowned crane, must be kept at a minimum temperature of 50 deg. F. (10 deg. C.). The floor of the shed must be covered with a thick layer of sand or sawdust.

European and demoiselle cranes are best kept in pairs. A large park can hold several pairs of demoiselle cranes, but not of the European variety, which needs rather more space. It is quite possible to keep a whole colony of crowned cranes, provided we realise that two of the birds might pair and turn against the rest.

All cranes are both carnivorous and herbivorous. They are fed on a mixture of soaked maize, soaked wheat, cooked and raw minced meat, soaked dog biscuit, and bread, cut up into small pieces. Water should be given in deep, almost completely filled bowls, in which the birds can fully immerse their bills.

The smaller the area, the more varied the birds' diet must be. They will not need elaborate feeding, as described above, if they are kept in large parks, where they can forage for themselves. Cranes are always in search of food and devour worms and insects of every kind. It is often amazing what trouble these giant birds will take over the tiniest worms.

All these cranes are easily obtained and are comparatively cheap. Other, more expensive cranes are also occasionally offered for sale, amongst them the gigantic sarus crane from India and the handsome Stanley crane, or paradise crane, from South Africa. Sarus cranes, especially, are keen burrowers and can do a lot of damage in a garden.

Cranes may breed easily if they can enjoy full freedom and are not locked up at night. In spring, they look for a secluded corner, where they build their simple nest from grasses, moss and small twigs. The clutch consists of one or two eggs, which are guarded and hatched by both parents. The incubating period of the European crane lasts *c.* 31 days, that of crowned and demoiselle cranes 22 days and 28 days respectively. Since the eggs are laid at intervals of two days, and are sat on from the first day, the young will not hatch simultaneously. The young frequently cannot get on together and each parent therefore takes charge of one chick.

When the young are hatched, a difficult problem might arise. Their parents normally feed them on small live worms or insects which they dangle before them in their bills. The chick sits in front of its parent, waiting to be fed. Occasionally, the parents cannot learn how to pass to their young the food which we give to them, the parents, and the young birds may die of hunger unless there is enough natural food available. It is therefore sometimes better to rear cranes by hand. This can be quite difficult, because the chicks will not sit still, always want to roam with their parents or foster-parents, and have to be warmed and comforted when they are cold or wet. Fortunately, they accept rearing lamps. During the first days, it is necessary to give them comparatively small portions *very often*—as their parents would—and to see that they go near the lamp. The rearing food consists at first of finely chopped hard-boiled egg, ants' eggs, chopped earthworms and mealworms, cut-up meat, small pieces of fish and bread crumbs. Mealworms and ants' eggs are later omitted. After three weeks, the little birds will already eat grain. If they are kept in a small enclosure, they also need green food. At three months, they begin to be independent.

Cranes that have lived in captivity for some time occasionally become vicious towards strangers. They must therefore be fenced in in such a way that strangers cannot get near them accidentally. The fence should be between 5 and 6 ft. high. Hand-reared cranes often become very friendly, but even those caught as mature birds frequently lose their initial shyness and perform their charming dances, in which male and female call to each other, flap their wings and bow. According to the late Duke of Bedford, who kept every possible variety of bird at liberty on his estates at Tavistock and Woburn, these dances are not a form of display, but merely an expression of well-being. Cranes can live to a great age. An Australian crane at the Berlin Zoo was at least 46 years old at the time of its death.

The Author will never forget 'Hans', a crane kept by a former warden of the great wild life sanctuary on the Schorfheide, north of Berlin. 'Hans' had come into the owner's possession as a sick bird with an injured wing and stayed on his farm for some time. In summer, when the wild cranes arrived, he went out into the swamps and lakes and often stayed away for months. But he regularly returned in autumn and ruled the roost amongst the domestic poultry until the following spring.

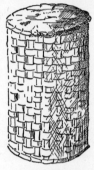

Cranes are sent in tall baskets or boxes, where they can stand upright on the journey. The floor of the box or basket should be covered with chaff and not long hay or straw, in which the birds might

Travelling-basket for cranes

entangle themselves. Strange cranes should not travel together because they sometimes fight savagely in a small space.

If we keep birds, our friends and neighbours sometimes imagine that we can nurse anything back to health as long as it has feathers. Fully grown birds brought to us have usually hurt themselves against a wall, etc., were fired at, or are in a very exhausted condition. They may also have been soaked by heavy rain and are thus temporarily disabled.

If a bird has merely had a soaking, put it into a dark cardboard box, with a soft woollen rag at the bottom, and keep it in a warm—but not excessively hot—place. When the storm has passed, and the bird is dry again, it can safely be restored to freedom.

Occasionally—indeed quite frequently—such birds fall into our hands in spring or autumn, during the migrating season, when they have grown tired and have settled in the wrong place. This is often the fate of aquatic birds, such as coots, moorhens and divers; they mistake a wet road, or the reflection on a freshly tarred roof, for water, settle there, and are so surprised that they 'stay put' and are run over, or are killed by a cat. With luck, they might be discovered by a bird-lover. If they are uninjured, simply take them to the next stream or pond, where they will find everything they need.

It is more difficult to help birds that have become exhausted through hunger. Swallows, and the very similar—but not related—swifts, are often found in a very weak condition after prolonged rains. They will need food immediately, so hold the bird in one hand, gently open its bill from the side, and push fresh or moistened dried ants' eggs down its throat with a pair of tweezers, until it has to swallow. To put down a bowl of food would be no use at all, since the birds are used to snapping at flying insects and would therefore not associate a bowl with feeding. They would merely starve to death if they were not fed forcibly. This applies also to many other birds. The food we give them is often very different from their natural diet and would not be taken voluntarily. When the swallows, or swifts, have regained their strength, they can be let out again as soon as there is an interval between rains.

In winter, we frequently find aquatic birds whose home has frozen. They must also be fed forcibly to prevent exhaustion, or to help them regain their strength. No bird understands that it must eat to survive, and therefore it must not be assumed that it will start eating on its own initiative. This only happens very rarely, or not at all. If it does happen, it is usually too late, because the body is too weak to digest anything. Forcible feeding is therefore essential. As soon as it has recovered, the bird can be released again at a suitable place near some water. It would be too risky to let it find a pond or stream by itself.

Injured birds must be examined very carefully. If there are only skin or flesh wounds the bird is merely kept in a quiet secluded spot and forcibly fed on the diet described for the various species; small quantities should be given fairly frequently. Birds recover very quickly, so long as they have proper food. If the wounds are large and gaping, we can either clamp them together ourselves or have it done by a veterinary surgeon or at a dispensary or clinic for sick animals (there is one in most towns). Certainly, we should not perform even the simplest operation unless we have some experience.

Broken wings or legs are unfortunately very common. If the broken or injured wing is still more or less in its normal shape, shows no pieces of bone projecting from wounds and does not dangle or drag, leave the bird alone. If it hangs limply and looks quite lifeless, set it carefully, put it into small wooden splints and tie it up with gauze to give it support. Unfortunately, the injury often swells under the bandage, gangrene sets in and the damaged limb drops off. The loss of a wing or leg only rarely prevents the bird from living a good many years longer. One of the Author's silver pheasants lost a leg in an accident, recovered quickly, and still walks about on the stump as if nothing had happened. A good rest in a quiet spot and regular feeding are, of course, also essential in the case of injured birds.

Birds that have flown against a wall, etc., usually suffer badly

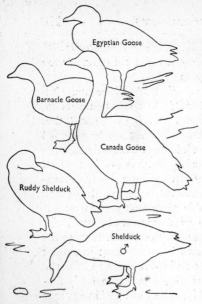

Egyptian Goose
Barnacle Goose
Canada Goose
Ruddy Shelduck
Shelduck ♂

Egyptian Goose, *Alopochen aegyptiacus.* 28 in. Tropical Africa. **Barnacle Goose,** *Branta leucopsis.* 26 in. Greenland, Spitzbergen. The Brent Goose, *Branta bernicla,* 23 in., from the Arctic regions of Europe and America, has a black head and neck, with a small white patch on the throat, and is otherwise dark above and lighter below. **Canada Goose,** *Branta canadensis.* 40 in. North America. Many varieties; the bird in the illustration, *Branta canadensis canadensis,* from western Canada to Utah, is frequently found in captivity. Other breeds are also offered for sale from time to time, amongst them the very small Hutchins' Goose, *Branta canadensis hutchinsii* from north-eastern Canada. **Ruddy Shelduck,** *Tadorna ferruginea,* also called *Casarca f.* 24 in. Southern Spain and North Africa, temperate zone of Asia and south-eastern Europe to Manchuria. **Shelduck,** *Tadorna tadorna.* 24 in. The female without the red knob on the bill and with a narrower band round breast and shoulders. British Isles, Europe to China and Japan.

---

from concussion. They sit about, completely stunned and unable to fly, but recover sooner or later, if they have survived the first few minutes after the accident. Small birds must be fed forcibly, if they have gone without food for half a day, and larger birds after a day. They must be kept alone in a quiet place, since other birds might disturb them or even peck at their heads. Birds with brain injuries often take to cage life rapidly. They get used to their surroundings during convalescence, when their faculties are not yet fully restored, and often have no desire to travel when they have fully recovered.

But injured or half-starved birds are not the bird-lover's only problem. What can he do when his birds are ill? Sickness is noticeable enough: the affected bird is less lively, is puffed

Flamingo, *Phoenicopterus ruber antiquorum.* 50 in. Mediterranean, Africa, southern Asia. **Red Flamingo,** *Phoenicopterus ruber ruber.* 50 in. Coasts and islands of the Caribbean. The South American Flamingo, *Phoenicopterus ruber chilensis,* from Peru to Chile, has grey legs with red joints. **Demoiselle Crane,** *Anthropoides virgo.* 40 in. Southern Europe to western China. **Grey Crane,** *Grus grus,* also called *Melagornis g.* 46 in. Europe, western Asia. Lilford's Crane, *Grus grus lilfordi,* from China and Japan, is lighter. **Crowned Crane,** *Balearica regulorum.* 40 in. South Africa. Closely related forms occur throughout the African grasslands. The West African Crowned Crane, *Balearica pavonina,* has a black neck and some red in the lower portion of the bare skin patch on the head. All crested cranes need the same food and accommodation; none are hardy.

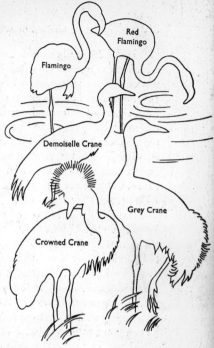

up and may even allow itself to be caught. Amongst the undomesticated species, treatment usually comes too late in a serious illness. Absolute cleanliness, light, the right amount of sunshine, and protection against draughts and excessive heat are the best safeguards against the all too common diseases resulting from colds. The right food, given in the right quantity, prevents digestive trouble, and a varied diet makes deficiency diseases unlikely. The birds will then stay healthy and will live far longer than when at liberty. Longevity and successful breeding pairs are the most reliable testimony to the owner's methods.

A bird suffering from a cold is kept in a warm and sheltered place. Digestive troubles can be due to internal parasites. Every spring, before the breeding season begins, pheasants should therefore be de-wormed with a reliable preparation obtainable from pet shops. One of the worst parasites, against which no adequate cure has been discovered so far, is gape-worm (*Syngamus tracheus*). It can wreak havoc amongst young peafowl and pheasants; the birds suffer from increasing breathlessness and slowly perish. Wild sparrows are amongst the most dangerous carriers of this terrible disease and must therefore be kept out of the aviary as far as possible. Professor A. Ghigi, the great Italian authority on pheasants, has suggested that gape-worm in its early stages can be cured with garlic. Other parasites, such as mites and scab, are easily cured with present-day methods.

Every bird that is not quite healthy should at once be isolated in a cage of its own, where it can be observed and given the necessary attention. A small bird that stops eating must be fed forcibly, if it is not to lose strength very quickly.

A sick bird that is brought in should also be isolated, since many diseases, amongst them cholera or fowl pest, are highly contagious and can easily be transmitted through carriers, such as insects, etc. Each patient could be a carrier and thus a danger to one's entire collection. Even wild birds may be carriers of ornithosis, or psittacosis, as it used to be called. This disease is dealt with at greater length in the chapter on parrots.

The number of diseases that affect one's birds is legion. It is unlikely that any veterinary surgeon will have specialised in them. But many bird periodicals contain advertisements for all kinds of preparations, whose names and composition are subject to fashion as much as anything else. Good, and even surprising, results are reported from time to time; but prevention is better, and very much cheaper, than any cure.

Some birds moult once or twice every year. This is always a critical time. All European birds change their plumage once or twice a year throughout several weeks or even months, usually from July to September. Tropical breeds are not so closely tied to specific dates. Several species have a second moult, usually in mid-winter. This applies particularly to migrants—such as the icterine warblers who winter in the tropics. If the moult is very strenuous, the birds appear dejected and less lively than usual. Give them, therefore, a rich, varied diet and take great care to protect them against draughts and dampness. The bird's natural reserves, fully taken up with forming the new plumage, will be at their lowest. Birds moulting in winter should have a small dose of ultra-violet rays every day; this treatment will help any bird during the short days of winter.

Night migrants often damage their feathers very badly in the dark when the migrating urge is at its strongest. Therefore, put a small lamp near the cage or bird-room at night, although there is no need for such a precaution near an out-door aviary. But all night migrants must be segregated from other birds—whether indoors or out—during the migrating season, when they can cause a great deal of disturbance at night.

When given fledglings to rear, first ascertain what birds they are. The young of insessorial birds (whose young keep to their nests) should be put into an old nest, which is then placed in a cardboard box. If the quills have already burst through, and the first feathers are showing, the birds will only need artificial heat in very cold weather. Simply place a hot-water bottle above the box, leave a small gap, and make sure from time to time that the birds are comfortable and warm. If the birds are still bare, artificial heat is absolutely essential. An electric bulb is an excellent source of heat, as are numerous other devices—including a type of hot plate, which creates exactly the right temperature, i.e. body heat—manufactured by firms supplying poultry breeders. Birds breeding in hollows are kept in a very dark place; birds breeding in the open need light, provided they are no longer bare. Food must be given very often, in small quantities, since the birds cannot control their appetite. If young song-birds will not open their little beaks readily to be fed, open them with the utmost care and feed forcibly. Fresh ants' eggs—or moistened, dried eggs, if no fresh ones are available—a few cut-up mealworms and chopped yolk of egg will suit most of our native insectivorous birds and also most seed-eaters, such as finches and buntings. Other birds should have the food recommended for their breed in the appropriate chapter.

As soon as the young bird is fully fledged and wants to leave its nest-substitute, put it into a cage and continue feeding it until it will take enough food without any encouragement. This development is hastened by putting the rearing food into a bowl, and by either passing this bowl to the bird or by hand-feeding the bird from it.

Most native and foreign song-birds keep to their nests for a comparatively short time—mostly not above two to three weeks —and are fed by their parents for another three or four weeks, unless the mother is again laying or incubating. Orphaned nestlings can usually be reared with a little care—all they need are frequent meals of the right kind, and warmth.

The young of autophagous birds (whose young follow them around, like ground birds and aquatic birds) are more of a problem. They not only need food and warmth, but also like to be taken for walks. Unless they have a great deal of attention, they grow very shy and pine away, especially if they are the sole members of a brood. The company of a brother or sister usually makes up for the missing parents.

An empty aquarium, with a layer of sand at the bottom and equipped with some source of artificial heat—an electric bulb or a heat cushion—is ideally suited for our purpose. Many chicks, particularly young gallinaceous birds, start eating without any instruction, although the example of a mother always helps. Once again, therefore, we must take on a mother's duties, cackle like an old hen, and use a small wooden stick to imitate her pecking and scratching amongst the food. Coots and cranes dangle the food before their young, until they take it from them. So it is necessary to hold it before them with a pair of tweezers and forcibly feed them at once, if they show no interest. This process has to be continued until they accept us in place of their parents. Sea-gulls gurgitate their food before giving it to their young. We put it before the young gulls and again feed them forcibly, if they show no interest. Later, the young autophagi are put into boxes, which can be left open at the top, although they must be covered with lids of wire-netting as soon as the young birds begin to flutter around. They can also be put into rearing coops (described in the chapter on pheasants) where they are left with a rearing lamp. Such a lamp is at first kept going all day; later—when the feathers have grown—only at night. Naturally, they must be inspected from time to time to ensure that all is well.

The younger a bird is the more likely it is to accept us in place of its parents. The young of our insessorial song-birds at first—for about 8 to 10 days—open their beaks to everything that comes near them, whether it is a parent, a cat, or a human being. They are therefore easy to feed at that stage; their parents, or their keeper, are not recognised until later. If we obtain them when they are a little older, we must feed them forcibly, until they accept us.

Young autophagous birds recognise their real or assumed parents within the first few days. They are quite willing to accept human beings, but it must be appreciated that most of them are a little frightened of anything very much larger than themselves. It is therefore a good idea to put them on the table in their coop, or box, so that we do not appear quite so large to them. The effect is almost instantaneous, and they get used to us very quickly. Often, their affection is almost embarrassing: they follow us everywhere and we must take great care not to step on them.

Hand-rearing is a matter of time and patience: if we lack these, we can try to put a young bird that has been brought to us into a nearby nest. This is mostly successful in the case of insessorial birds, if their feathers have not yet grown, if the difference in age is not too great, and if the foster-parents belong to a related species. Young blackbirds can be reared by song-thrushes, blue- or coal-tits. But if the young in the strange nest are almost fully-fledged, a bird cannot be placed there; the original inhabitants would leave at once.

Adoption is more difficult amongst autophagous birds. Families are already acquainted from the beginning and any new-comers would be pecked to death. The only possible foster-mothers are turkey hens or domestic hens, although even these may chase the little 'stranger' away or they may prefer their own offspring. It is therefore better to take the foster-mother's own brood away. The exchange should be made in the dark to avoid complications; it is also advisable to put the hen into a fairly small box, so that the young orphans can find her easily, and to stay with them until it is clear that all is well.

A young hand-reared bird is very much in need of attention when it becomes independent and learns to feed itself. It is the time when it normally leaves its parents. It will be very suspicious, easily frightened and inclined to go wild. If it is to be kept tame, it must be given a lot of attention and kept apart from members of its own species, amongst whom it would forsake us very soon.

The tip of the wing is removed at the point marked with a line. Bottom right: Pinioning a duckling

Hand-reared birds generally will not get used to freedom. A release is the equivalent of a death sentence. They are too tame, too friendly and cannot find their own food. If they cannot be kept they must be found another home.

Every bird-keeper must know how to stop his birds from flying away. They either have to be clipped or pinioned. If they are to be clipped, spread out one wing and cut off the first eight to ten flight feathers—counted from the outside, i.e. from the tip of the wing—close to the skin, taking care not to cut off any of the coverts, which are the small feathers covering the flight feathers or primaries. The feathers may grow again during the next moult and should be shortened while they are still growing, without, of course, damaging the quills containing the blood vessels. Pinioning can only be done by an experienced bird-keeper or a veterinary surgeon, as it is essential to know the structure of the wing thoroughly before venturing on this task. The long upper arm usually has comparatively short feathers. The lower arm, like the human, consists of two bones, and of one row of strong flight feathers and two rows of smaller feathers, the wing coverts. The continuation of the lower arm is the hand, consisting of three joints, as shown in the illustration. The largest of these three joints has a small feathered protuberance, the thumb, which must not be removed. Simply bind the wing tightly above the thumb and cut it with a very sharp pair of scissors in one movement. The wound is then cauterised with iodine. The bird will have lost

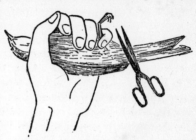

Birds must be held firmly, but extremely carefully, for trimming claws

two joints of its hand completely and a large portion of the third. Out of ten or eleven flight feathers, seven or eight will have been removed completely. If fewer are removed, some capacity for flight will have been retained. The tie is removed after several hours, or will fall off by itself. Great care must be taken to avoid a haemorrhage. Only one wing is pinioned.

Most bird-lovers will not be attracted by this operation. No pheasant hen that is likely to be attacked by the cock should be pinioned, nor should any of the more sedentary ducks. Undoubtedly, fully winged birds are more interesting, enjoy life more, and will therefore give us greater pleasure.

Every bird-lover likes his charges to be tame and friendly. Whether a bird is friendly and fond of us depends on many factors. If a sparrow that comes to us in the park, and will even eat out of our hand, is placed in a small cage, it may be mad with despair, flutter about, and may even die, unless it is restored to freedom. Placed in a fairly large aviary, it may soon be as friendly as in full freedom. The tameness of a sparrow is thus something very different from that of the blue-fronted Amazon, who appreciates our attention and likes to be fondled. The sparrow only comes to us to be fed, and stays with us because he is not afraid. The blue-fronted Amazon enjoys our company and accepts us for our own sake. A silver pheasant cock, by contrast, attacks us like an unleashed wild beast as soon as we enter the aviary. He does not fear us, but hates us and tries to drive us away. Here are three tame birds with completely different reactions.

The tameness of the sparrow is very widespread amongst the cage-birds. They normally flee from man and most are caught as adult birds. The terrible experience of being caught and handled is behind them, and we should try to make them forget it and to trust us. This depends partly on ourselves and partly on the bird's memory, which can be extremely good. Some blackbirds, caught by the Author for ringing, were still much shyer after a year than others. Even the reactions of birds of the same breed cannot be foretold.

New arrivals must be treated very gently. All excitement must be avoided, and they should be spoken to in a low and comforting voice. Many birds are very frightened of any silent creature. If we speak to them, they will feel very much safer. The cage should be slightly below shoulder level to make us appear less overpowering. The right choice of cage is very important. The Author once placed a pair of newly imported St. Helena waxbills in a 16 in. long cage. The birds remained extremely shy. A few days later, a 24-in. cage became vacant; the birds were moved and at once became tame and friendly. They probably felt that they could withdraw better in more spacious surroundings, which gave them a sense of security. On another occasion, the Author kept a pair of eagle owls in an aviary covering an area of 40 sq. yd. The sides were made of wire-netting. The birds seemed shy and frightened. When they were transferred to a smaller aviary measuring only 26 sq. yd., with a solid rear wall and sides that were solid half-way up, they at once became friendlier and even bred year after year; they, too, felt much more secure. Undoubtedly, box-cages are therefore suitable for many birds, who like to feel that they can hide somewhere.

Tameness and friendliness—and not only in birds—are often a form of cupboard love. If we stay near the birds for a few moments when we bring them their food in the mornings we can observe them torn between two emotions; they would like to eat, but are frightened of the monster who is standing nearby. Slowly, the bird learns that we are harmless and that he can eat in our presence. This development is hastened if we encourage him to take tit-bits, such as mealworms, if it is an insectivorous bird, directly from our hand or from a pair of tweezers.

Jays, and many predatory birds, are individualists and only pair during the breeding season. They are not likely to come to us. Birds normally living in a flock see in us a substitute for other birds and will take to us readily. This can be observed in siskins or many small parrots. But if we keep them in a flight-cage, bird-room or aviary, they will prefer their own company and will only come near us at feeding time.

Many chaffinches never take to cage life and will always resent and fear us, although they may become quite friendly in a large aviary. These birds cannot grasp that the pain they suffer when they fly against the bars can be avoided. They merely associate us with it, and their shyness increases, if anything, over the years. In an aviary, they do not fly against bars, therefore suffer no pain, and get used to us. In England, where wild birds cannot be kept in cages, unless they have been aviary-bred, such problems fortunately do not arise.

Robins and warblers take to cage life much quicker than chaffinches. The latter move towards the light, the former withdraw into the dark. The bars of the cage make them feel secure, like a curtain of leaves. Such birds would merely feel themselves in greater danger in a large cage.

Hand-reared birds do not have to get accustomed to us. The young bird is given food and warmth by his parents. He does not really know what they look like. Normally, they are the first creatures he meets. After some time, he learns to recognise them, although some birds have an innate knowledge of a few —though by no means all—characteristics of their parents. Pheasants and ducks know their mothers' calls—but not their looks—from the first moment. We can, therefore, easily make them used to us, if we sit down near them, warm them and call them in the manner of an old hen. They also accept a foster-mother, and even know her voice when they have been kept with her in a confined space for the first few days. Here, innate and acquired knowledge—the call and the appearance—are closely linked.

Similarly, birds learn to recognise their enemies. Insessorial birds start learning when their feathers begin to show. Auto-phagous birds learn from the very beginning; the warning calls of their parents teach them who their enemies are. Insessorial birds go through a period of distrust and suspicion immediately after they have left their parents. They generally avoid human beings or larger animals, although we can occasionally teach them that they are harmless or, like their keeper, even part of their surroundings.

The robin is an important exception to this rule. As soon as any large animal approaches, he rushes near to catch some of the insects stirred up by it. If we give him a mealworm each time we approach his cage, we will confirm him in his association of large creatures with food and will soon gain his affection.

Hand-reared birds accept their keeper as a parent; they may later look on him as an associate, as a substitute for the missing flock. The hand-reared budgerigar, sparrow or jackdaw sees in us another budgerigar, sparrow or jackdaw, however embarrassing we may find this at times. Budgerigars will sit on our shoulders and pinch our ears, sparrows may try to build their nest in our clothes; being not only 'sparrows', but also large, they consider us a home as well as a companion.

A hand-reared bird may see in us a possible mate or rival, who must be chased from his territory. Even a very small bird sometimes attacks his keeper fearlessly. There is little we can do without hurting him, and we must suffer as understanding bird-lovers when a kestrel scratches our scalp to drive us away.

Birds that pair for life, like the larger parrots, geese and cranes, frequently get very attached to their keepers. If they have been hand reared, they consider themselves 'married' to us, will defend us against other birds and human beings, and will even display for us. Such birds sometimes show no interest in other birds of their own kind, get depressed in their company, and cry for their keeper. They may even attack other birds and we should therefore keep them under observation for some time, if there is not to be a tragedy. Usually, such renegades return to the fold. We can make this easier for them by keeping them near their future companions in an enclosure divided by wire-netting. The birds can see each other, but cannot quarrel. They soon calm down and get gradually accustomed to each other's company.

It is often difficult to match breeding pairs. Every breeder knows that a male and a female do not necessarily make a pair. Birds arbitrarily thrown together are often not interested in each other. The best food, the most luxurious nest-boxes, fail to make them build a nest or to show any inclination for breeding. Even if they do breed, it is not at all certain whether they will stay on the nest, rear their young and not fail somewhere in their duty as prospective parents.

It is always advisable to pick for breeding those birds that show an interest in each other when they are still in the flock. This applies particularly to foreign finches and parrots. The more domesticated a bird has become, the less fussy it will be in its choice of mate, as illustrated by the canary and zebra finch, bengalese and budgerigar, but especially by domestic poultry and ducks.

If the birds are more interested in birds of other breeds than in their own kind—which is not unusual amongst hand-reared birds—segregate them as quickly as possible, since hybridisation is only very rarely successful amongst wild birds. Domesticated, or semi-domesticated, breeds form an exception: canaries, bengalese and zebra finches cross without great difficulty, if a male of the wild form is paired with a female of the domesticated variety. Many of our native seed-eaters have been crossed with canaries, particularly those closest to the serin—the wild form of the canary—such as siskins, linnets, goldfinches and redpolls. It is more difficult with distant relations, like other finches and buntings. Bengalese and zebra finches are crossed with other foreign finches; domestic ducks cross with many wild ducks; domestic hens cross with pheasants. But it is, as a rule, better to avoid hybrids. They are very hard to sell and are often sterile, unless the parents belong to closely related breeds.

Prospective breeders must remember that all the actions connected with breeding are innate. They were not taught to the bird and cannot be adapted to changed circumstances. A weaver will try to build his magnificent hanging nest in the cage no less than in the African steppes; pigeons' nests are as messy in the aviary as outside; the mallard is as bad a father on our pond as he would be in freedom. A bird is primarily concerned with leading a normal life in captivity. Budgerigars nest in hollows, and will therefore be content with any hole, whether it is in a disused concrete drain, in a tree or in a nest-box. Each bird also seems to know how to place its nest—it is put into the right position, whether in a fork or in a corner, although the setting might be very different from nature. But the bird will use any material to build its nest, even strips of silver paper.

It is therefore very important that birds should not only have the right materials, but also suitable nesting sites. Siskins must have thick shrubs, where they can find cover. There is no need to plant those bushes in which they would build their nests in freedom. Support and protection are all they need. What kind of shrub we give them is immaterial.

It is often said that birds leave their nests, or even their young, if we touch them. This is a very widespread error. We must simply not frighten the parent birds and must approach the nest very gently.

Birds cannot recognise their eggs and will try to hatch any similar object. They are also ignorant of the number of their eggs, or even of their young. If an egg, or a chick, falls out, it is lost. No bird bothers to get it back. Autophagous birds, like pheasants, are not worried if one, or several, of their brood are missing. A domestic hen does not look for her young, unless she is alarmed by their chirping. She does not notice it when several of her young are missing, although she can tell them apart from strange chicks. The young must therefore be counted frequently.

Bird-lovers repeatedly experience that their charges cannot adapt themselves to change. A goose that has escaped from its enclosure never appreciates that it cannot return through the wire-netting, and will take hours to realise that it can cross it with a flap of its wings. It is used to getting through undergrowth and will never learn that wire-netting is impenetrable. Many birds cannot find the opening in their cage when they have been let out for a while and want to return to their feeding bowl. They fly against the bars and only find the door by accident. Birds are incapable of learning by observation, and it must be appreciated that they are therefore exposed to many dangers.

Indeed, birds are creatures of habit far more than we are. Any change in the cage or aviary can upset them to the highest degree. It may seem a small thing to us to move a perch or a feeding bowl, or to change feeding times, but a bird's well-being can be profoundly affected by it. Many birds cannot eat properly for days when the position of the cage has been changed. A re-arrangement of its perches may mean that it has to reorganise all its movements. All the trouble it has taken to settle in its little prison—for that, after all, is the nature of a cage—will have been in vain. Many birds have been unwittingly sacrificed for the sake of such foolish innovations. A thrush or a shama can smash all its flight feathers because it is frightened of a strange object, perhaps a harmless vase, that has been put near its cage.

The peace of an entire flight-cage, bird-room or aviary can be upset because the inmates suddenly have to find new sleeping places. Even a perfectly peaceful new-comer may cause great upheaval amongst old residents, who now have to establish some relationship to the new arrival. Therefore change the accommodation of the birds as infrequently as possible, restrain any urge for frequent re-decorations, and limit activities to feeding and cleaning-out.

Most birds—apart from a few exceptions—dislike being picked up or stroked. It is always a painful experience for them. They probably feel as if some wild beast held them in its claws. Only some species nesting in hollows, and therefore used to a confined space, behave differently. If the birds' claws must be trimmed, do this as quickly as possible, taking care to catch them without any undue chase. Those people who want outlets for their emotions, who want animals that can be carried about and fondled, should get a cat or a dog. It is demanding too much of birds to expect them to appreciate our kind intentions and to reciprocate our affection.

It is often suggested it is cruel to keep birds. Such an accusation cannot be treated lightly. There is no question that it is wrong to consider an animal or bird merely as a source of amusement, to be put into a cage, where it will sing and talk in solitude, and to be discarded when it suits us. Obviously, we have a great responsibility towards the birds we keep and we must make them as comfortable as we can. Keeping birds inevitably means a lot of work, a certain amount of expense and a sense of devotion. We cannot just go on holiday without making arrangements for feeding and cleaning, and we cannot release birds when they have begun to bore us.

Many animals have become almost extinct to-day. Experiments of all kinds are made daily, vast stretches of land are cultivated or built up, rivers are drained and sea-shores polluted. It seems slightly hypocritical to accuse bird-fanciers of cruelty under such circumstances. But we must remember that it can indeed be cruel to own birds if they are not looked after properly and if their cages are too small, of the wrong shape and are kept in the wrong place.

Not everybody is able to keep cranes, parrots and swans at liberty, like the late Duke of Bedford. His estates at Tavistock and Woburn Abbey—the latter within easy reach of London and open to the public—included woods and paddocks inhabited by birds of every kind. A man of the highest principles, full of reverence for every living creature, he looked on birds as individuals, whose moods and needs had to be carefully studied. He proved that it is possible to give birds almost complete freedom, if sufficient trouble is taken at the beginning. His innumerable contributions to bird literature are not mere treatises on ornithological species, but almost biographies of dear friends. Yet he did not endow birds with human qualities they do not possess. He simply studied them, not with a cold, diabolic and Pavlovian detachment, but with the selfless love and conscientiousness that had governed his entire life. His Woburn estate became a sanctuary for wild animals from all over the world, amongst them deer, bison and the last surviving Przewalski's horse in Europe. A ceaseless worker for peace, he was anxious to protect his fellow creatures—both men and animals—from extinction, a fate that appears not altogether unlikely to-day.

More and more tropical birds are imported, and even bred. Certainly, the beginner can study all kinds of books and journals on this subject—by no means without excellent results —but nothing can replace experience gained in the course of many years. It is best to learn from a bird-keeper of many years' standing. There are numerous organisations with branches in most large towns throughout the country.

Periodicals include *Birds Illustrated*, *Fur and Feather*, *Cage Birds* and other journals. Some of the best-known books on bird-keeping are *Parrots and Parrot-like Birds*, by the late Duke of Bedford, undoubtedly one of the greatest experts on parrots. W. T. Greene's *Parrots in Captivity*, published in 1884, is now almost unobtainable and has become a collector's item. *Aviculture*, published in 1936 by the Avicultural Society, includes a number of contributions by leading authorities. It covers almost every bird in existence, but is also very difficult to obtain. Witherby's, the editors and publishers of *The Handbook of British Birds*, 5 vols., have also published a booklet on cage-birds. Cassell's *Pet and Livestock* series includes a number of useful volumes on parrots, British birds, ducks and pigeons, etc.

One of the great standard works on finches, Butler's *Foreign Finches in Captivity*, published at the end of the last century, contains many references to Dr. Karl Russ, one of the best-known German authors on cage-birds. Russ's *Handbuch für Vogelliebhaber* was first published in 1870 and has had many editions since. Russ, who was born in West Prussia in 1833, wrote a series of books on bird-keeping and was also the founder of the famous German periodical *Gefiederte Welt*. He died in 1899. His successor on the *Gefiederte Welt* was Karl Neunzig, originally the illustrator of Russ's books. He brought out a new three-volume edition of the *Handbuch der Vogelpflege*, which did more than anything else to enhance the reputation of German bird-keepers. Neunzig's bird-rooms at times contained as many as 300 inhabitants. He was an outstanding bird painter and a man of almost unsurpassed experience in his own sphere.

The list of bird-lovers, of great bird illustrators, of nature poets and of ornithologists of repute could be increased indefinitely. To-day they all seem like the champions of sanity and of the things that are worthwhile, in a world that is becoming increasingly uglier and more mechanised.

INDEX

The numbers in **bold type** denote the *page numbers* of illustrations